NATURE
CONSERVANCY
COUNCIL

Vulnerable concentrations of birds in the North Sea

SEABIRDS AT SEA TEAM

EUROPEAN YEAR
OF THE ENVIRONMENT

Mark L Tasker and Michael W Pienkowski
Seabirds at Sea Team
Chief Scientist Directorate
Nature Conservancy Council

Preface

This document forms part of the product of the second phase (1983—1986) of the Seabirds at Sea research programme. The programme was started in 1979 and was designed primarily to find which areas of the North Sea were particularly important for seabirds. The programme is now in its third phase (which includes survey work to the west of Great Britain). Two major, and numerous smaller, reports have been published detailing results of the work (see Main additional sources of information) and further analyses are in preparation.

Erratum

On maps for June to May (pp 15-37), Easterly degrees longitude should read 1 to 12, not as shown 2 to 13.

Oystercatchers

Acknowledgements

The various phases of the Seabirds at
Sea programme have spanned eight
years (1979—1987). These phases have
been sponsored by both the oil industry
and Government: the Department of
Transport's Marine Pollution Control
Unit, the Department of Energy, the
Department of the Environment, Esso
Petroleum Co. Ltd., BP Petroleum
Development Ltd., BP International Ltd.,
Shell UK Ltd., the United Kingdom
Offshore Operators' Association and the
Nature Conservancy Council.

A full list of individuals in these and
other organisations who contributed to
the Seabirds at Sea project may be found
in Tasker *et al.* (1987). Derek R Langslow
initiated the second phase of the project
and chaired its steering group and we
are particularly grateful also to Andy
Webb for his help throughout this phase.

This document uses also information
from the Seabird Colony Register
(NCC/Seabird Group); National
Wildfowl Counts (Wildfowl Trust under
contract to NCC); Birds of Estuaries
Enquiry (British Trust for Ornithology/
NCC/Royal Society for the Protection of
Birds); Winter Shorebird Count (BOEE/
Wader Study Group); Moray Firth
Seabirds at Sea study (RSPB under
contract to Britoil plc).

Further unpublished information was
supplied by S. Asbirk, H. Baptist,
G.C. Boere, C.J. Camphuysen,
F. Danielsen, J. Durinck, T. Nygard,
H. Skov and J.A. van der Ven (IWRB).

Drafts were read and commented on
by L.H. Campbell, C.J. Camphuysen,
F. Danielsen, B.O. Dowsett, J. Durinck,
C.A. Galbraith, R. Mitchell, M.J. Nugent,
Th. Piersma, R.P. Prys-Jones, D.G. Salmon,
H. Skov, D.A. Stroud, W. Wynn-Williams.
Any remaining errors and omissions are
entirely the responsibility of the authors.

S. Wallace drew the maps.

We thank S.D. Collinge, P.H. Oswald,
R.A. Schofield and A. Webb for help in
the production of this document.

Department of Transport

Department of Energy

Esso

BP

Shell

Introduction

The North Sea supports several internationally important populations of seabirds. These birds use the surrounding coastline to breed and feed in adjacent waters. In winter some of them migrate southwards, but other seabirds that breed further north may replace them. Large numbers of shorebirds and waterfowl that breed in other areas as widespread as arctic Canada and Siberia move to the shores of the North Sea for the non-breeding season so taking advantage of the comparatively mild climate and good feeding conditions. The coastline of eastern Britain forms an extensive boundary to the North Sea, while part of the United Kingdom's continental shelf extends over approximately half of the sea's area. The United Kingdom therefore has a particular responsibility for the conservation of the birds of the North Sea, especially since any birds using the area do not recognise international boundaries and neither does pollution.

The Nature Conservancy Council (NCC) is statutorily required to provide advice on developments which may affect nature conservation in Great Britain. The development of the offshore oil industry raised fears that oil pollution might increase and have an adverse effect on the birds of the North Sea. In order to determine whether such fears were well founded, NCC established the Seabirds at Sea Team in 1979 with the objective of surveying the North Sea to discover important areas for seabirds. This project was inevitably expensive and support was sought from other organisations. Funding was forthcoming from the Marine Pollution Control Unit (now part of the Department of Transport and formerly of Trade) which is responsible for ameliorating the effects of any oil spill; the Department of Energy (responsible for the licensing of offshore oil and gas exploration and production); and those sections of the offshore oil and gas industry committed to careful planning of any developments. Surveying has continued since 1979, and this document represents one of the products of this project.

This document gathers together many diverse sources of information on the birdlife of the North Sea and assesses which sectors might hold birds particularly vulnerable to oil or other

Table 1

Numbers of seabirds breeding around the North Sea: see Tasker *et al.* (1987) for further details. Figures are pairs or apparently occupied sites unless otherwise stated. The proportion of the world population of the species or subspecies believed to breed in the North Sea is also indicated: * = more than 1%, ** = more than 10%, *? = possibly more than 1%, insufficient information on world population, S = proportion of subspecies.

Red-throated diver	800 **S	Herring gull	237 100 *S
Fulmar	308 000 *S	Great black-backed gull	24 400 **
Manx shearwater[1]	250	Kittiwake	415 400 *
Storm petrel[1]	1—5 000 *	Sandwich tern	30 500 *S
Leach's petrel[1]	1—500	Roseate tern	36
Gannet	43 800 **	Common tern	61 500
Cormorant	2 200	Arctic tern	74 700
Shag	19 800 **	Little tern	2 300
Arctic skua	3 200 *	Guillemot[3]	680 400 **S
Great skua	7 300 **	Razorbill[3]	73 100 **
Black-headed gull[2]	110 000	Black guillemot[4]	23 700 *?
Common gull	73 300	Puffin[5]	226 000 **S
Lesser black-backed gull	49 300 **		

Notes
1 Petrel and shearwater figures are very approximate.
2 There have been no censuses of Dutch coastal populations of black-headed gulls. This figure is therefore an underestimate.
3 Counts of individuals at breeding sites in early June.
4 Counts of individuals at breeding sites, conducted mostly in early morning in April.
5 A minimum number of individuals present. Occupied burrow counts, where conducted, have been multiplied by two and individual counts at other locations added to these.

These differing counting methods for different species have been developed as the best ways of obtaining consistent results for each species. These numbers are all less than the total numbers of birds present in the North Sea, as they do not include immatures and non-breeders.

pollution. This information is essential for contingency planning within the North Sea and has been designed for those concerned with the control of oil pollution. In collating this information, national boundaries have been ignored, hence the potential for damage has been assessed wherever possible on an international basis. This will inevitably cause some disagreement over the relative importance of areas, which we hope we have resolved successfully. The quality of data available for the North Sea is varied and we have indicated gaps in the survey; we apologise if any sources of information have been overlooked. Survey work by the United Kingdom continues and we would welcome any further data which become available from other sources.

For the purposes of this document, the North Sea includes all sea areas south of 62°N, west of continental Europe including the Skagerrak as far south as 57° 30′N (Frederikshaven—Onsala), north of 51°N and east of 5°W or mainland Britain, whichever is the further east (Figure 1).

The birds

The birds using the North Sea may be divided conveniently into three groups— offshore, inshore and coastal. The offshore group includes members of several families, most notably the petrels, gannets, gulls and auks. These birds breed on the coasts of the North Sea, but feed frequently far offshore. In the winter, many become less attached to the breeding site and may range considerable distances in search of food. The majority of these offshore birds that breed around the North Sea nest in northern Britain. Numbers of offshore (and some inshore) seabirds breeding on the coasts of the North Sea are shown in Table 1. Some of these numbers form important sections of the world populations of the species.

Inshore birds include the seaducks, divers, cormorants and terns. Some gull species and one auk (black guillemot) are included also in this group. These birds occur normally within sight of land, but may on occasion move to sites further offshore, especially in areas of shallow water. Substantial numbers of some of these types nest around the North Sea, but there is also considerable

immigration to the area during winter, particularly by seaduck. The southern North Sea holds the largest populations of many inshore birds.

Wading birds and ducks comprise the majority of the coastal category. Most of these birds feed typically on coastal mud- and sand-flats, but some feed on other intertidal areas. In the western North Sea, in addition to the estuaries, the beaches and low rocky areas of Orkney, Grampian, south-eastern Scotland, Northumberland and Kent are specially important. The North Sea is a particularly favourable area for these species owing to its large tidal amplitude and relatively mild climate, which prevents the mud-flats freezing for most of the winter. Most birds in this group breed to the north of the North Sea and move to the area in winter. Many species have a complex pattern of movements around the North Sea during winter, generally moving to milder western areas in the cold of midwinter.

Several mechanisms exist to conserve the assemblage of birds in the North Sea. There is a need to protect the habitats of the species. All coastal states around the North Sea have ratified or signed the Ramsar Convention on Wetlands of International Importance especially as Waterfowl Habitat. Under the

Razorbill

5

Figure 1

The North Sea showing localities
mentioned in the text.

Shetland Basin oil fields

Shetland

Norway

Sweden

Orkney

Fladden Ground

Caithness
Golspie
Dornoch Firth
Moray Firth
Cromarty Firth
Banff
Grampian
Beauly Firth
Ythan
Scotland
Tay
Eden
Montrose Basin
Firth of Forth
Tweed
Lindisfarne
Northumberland
Farne Islands
Newcastle
Teesmouth
Yorkshire
Humber
Wash
East Anglia
England
Orwell
Stour
Blackwater
Leigh
Thames
Medway
Kent

Skagerrak

Limfjord

Denmark

Jutland

Fisher Banks

Ekofisk

Dogger Bank

Outer Silver Pit

Wadden Sea
Amrun
Helgoland Bight
Grosser Knechtsand
Wadden Sea

Schleswig/
Holstein

West Germany

Wadden Sea

Netherlands

Southern Bight

Hamford Water
Colne
Dengie
Foulness

Delta Region/Netherlands

IJsselmeer

Belgium

English Channnel

convention, states accept a responsibility to protect wetlands and use them wisely. States are asked to designate internationally important individual wetlands. A wetland is considered internationally important if it regularly holds 1% of the individuals in a population of one species or subspecies of waterfowl or if it supports a total of over 20 000 waterfowl. The qualifying levels are given in Table 2. Throughout this report the term 'internationally important' refers to those sites which qualify under these internationally accepted criteria. Coastal sites in Britain already designated and those others, identified by NCC (as the governments advisors) as qualifying for designation and which will be put forward progressively for designation, are shown on Figure 2. This figure shows also those sites designated by other North Sea states. Many of these wetlands, together with other sites, qualify also as Special Protection Areas under the EC Directive on the Conservation of Wild Birds 1979. This Directive is concerned with the protection of vulnerable and other migratory birds and their habitats. Member States are required to designate and protect sites as necessary to conserve vulnerable and migratory birds. These areas are shown also in Figure 2. Although these are the ornithological sites of international importance, most of the coast is highly vulnerable to oil pollution, and further documentation of this is in progress. The present report is a summary of the main areas of vulnerability at sea, with coastal areas included for completeness.

Oil pollution

Pollution of the seas by oil has long been regarded as a threat to birdlife. The first recorded incident when birds were killed by oil in British waters was in 1907, when a wreck occurred on the Isles of Scilly. More recently, the wreck of the *Torrey Canyon* in 1967 brought the damage caused by oil firmly into the public consciousness. Within the North Sea, the rise of the offshore oil industry in the 1970s provoked some anxiety that the number of oil spills would increase, with consequent harm to bird populations. Undoubtedly oil has been spilt as a result of offshore production in the North Sea, but to date no damage to bird populations caused by oil from the platforms has been demonstrated. There remains the danger, however, that a large

Table 2

Qualifying levels for international importance of wetlands to waterfowl. Only those species whose population uses intertidal areas of the North Sea on a regular basis are included.

Species	Level	Species	Level
Mute swan	1 200	Goosander	750
Whooper swan	100	Oystercatcher	7 500
Pink-footed goose	1 000	Avocet	260
European white-fronted goose	2 000	Ringed plover	1 000
Dark-bellied brent goose	1 300	Golden plover	10 000
Light-bellied brent goose	40	Grey plover	800
Shelduck	1 250	Lapwing	20 000 *
Wigeon	5 000	Knot	3 500
Teal	2 000	Sanderling (passage)	500
Mallard	20 000 *	(winter)	150
Pintail	750	Purple sandpiper	?
Shoveler	1 000	Dunlin	20 000 *
Pochard	2 500	Ruff	10 000
Tufted duck	5 000	Snipe	10 000
Scaup	1 500	Black-tailed godwit	400
Eider	20 000 *	Bar-tailed godwit	5 500
Long-tailed duck	5 000	Whimbrel	500
Common scoter	10 000	Curlew	3 000
Velvet scoter	2 000	Spotted redshank	500
Goldeneye	2 000	Redshank	2 000
Smew	200	Greenshank	500
Red-breasted merganser	400	Turnstone	500

*The north-west European populations of these species exceeds two million but a site holding more than 20 000 waterfowl qualifies as internationally important by virtue of total numbers.

Figure 2

Location of sites on North Sea coasts notified under the 'Ramsar' Convention and as Special Protection Areas under the EC Directive on the Conservation of Wild Birds 1979. Sites in the United Kingdom that qualify under these two categories, and which will be put forward for designation are shown also.

■ SPA
□ Proposed SPA
● Ramsar sites
○ Proposed Ramsar sites

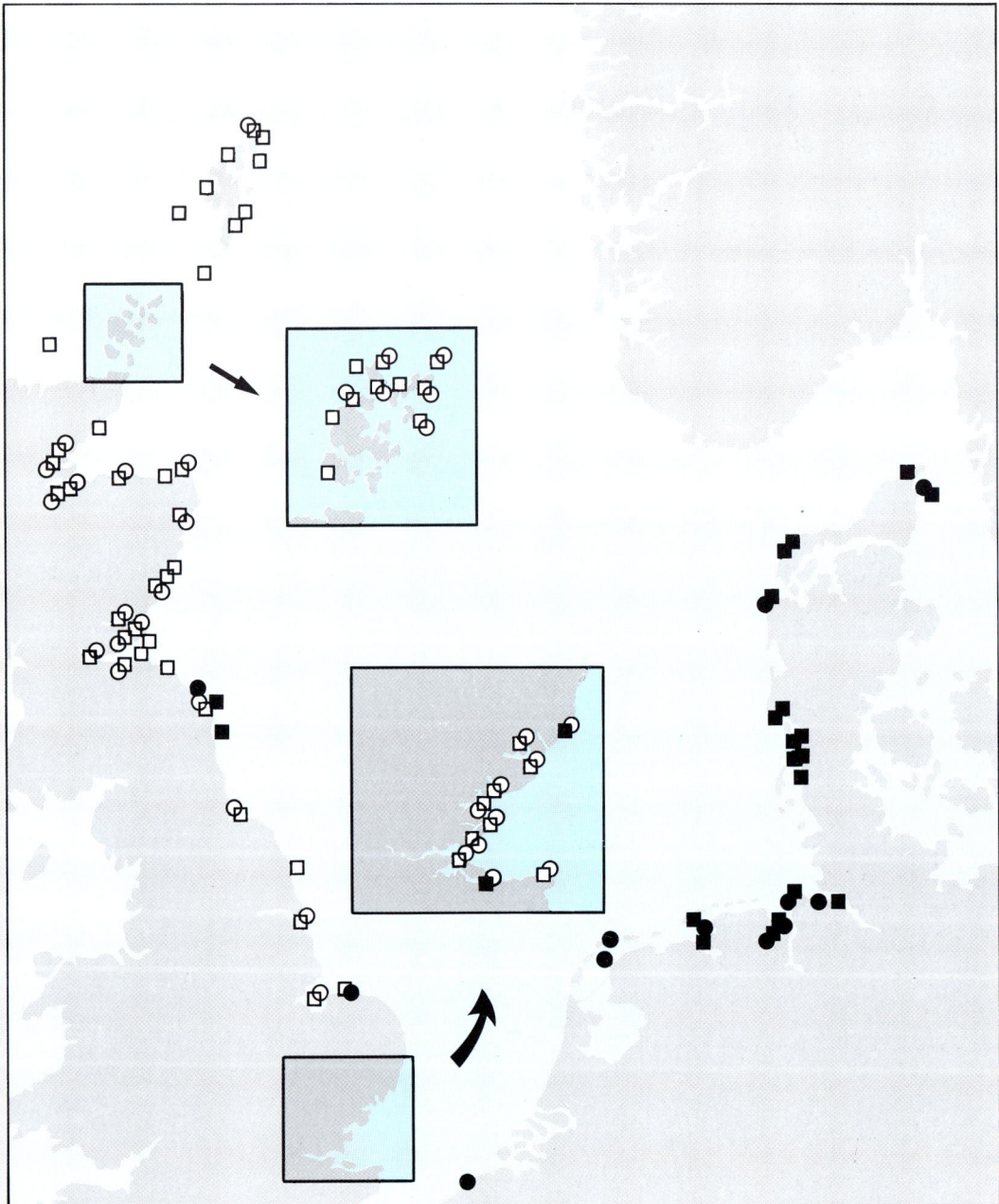

spill from an oil platform at certain times and places could cause major damage. The danger from shipping accidents is still present. The Seabirds at Sea project was initiated partly to investigate whether there are periods when birds might be at particular risk from spills and conversely to determine periods of least vulnerability when any risky oil-related operations could occur with least likelihood of danger to bird populations should an accidental oil spill occur.

The vulnerability of seabirds to surface-borne pollution—often oil—depends on a variety of factors. King & Sanger (1979), in a study on seabirds in Alaska, compiled an 'oil vulnerability index' by scoring 20 factors on a five-point scale. These factors included the size of the breeding population, the amount of time spent on the water during the year, threats from other sources, and the proportion of the year spent in the study area. The present study categorised species occurring in the North Sea on the basis of amount of time spent on the water and the importance of the area to the world population of the species. The species were divided into three categories of vulnerability—very high, high and moderate (Table 3).

Vulnerability of many species varies through the year. A number of species undergo a simultaneous total flight-feather moult at some stage of the year. These birds are confined to the surface of the water (or to mudbanks at low tide) for the period of flightlessness. This adds to the species' vulnerability at this time of year. Some species gather in a few restricted areas during this moult. For example, in late summer a very high proportion of the north-west European population of shelduck gathers on the German Wadden Sea to moult. This puts much of the population of this species at risk from a single oil spill.

Guillemots and razorbills are much more widely dispersed in winter than they are during the summer and early autumn. In summer, the breeding birds are confined to an area close to the colony by the need to incubate their egg(s) or obtain food for their chick(s). In early autumn, a large part of the North Sea populations of these species gathers off eastern Scotland during the moult period. The consequences of a pollution incident to a major colony or the moult area during one of these critical periods would be much more serious than at other times of year.

Those species of moderate vulnerability to oil pollution spend much of their time either on land or in the air over the sea. Several gulls, for example, obtain much of their food at sea from whole or parts of fish discarded from

Table 3

Vulnerability to oil pollution of species of birds in the North Sea: W = substantial period of life spent on water surface; P = North Sea important for large proportion of the world population of the species; R = species rare on a world basis.

Very high	High	Moderate
Red-throated diver (W)	Sooty shearwater	Fulmar
Black-throated diver (W)	Manx shearwater	Storm petrel
Great northern diver (W)	Gannet (P)	Little gull
Shag (W, P)	Cormorant (W)	Black-headed gull
Scaup (W)	Kittiwake	Common gull
Eider (W)	Great skua (P)	Lesser black-backed gull (P)
Common scoter (W,P)	Little auk (W)	Herring gull
Velvet scoter (W)	Little tern	Great black-backed gull (P)
Long-tailed duck (W)		Sandwich tern
Red-breasted merganser (W)	Shorebirds in the breeding	Arctic tern
Goldeneye (W)	season, some species on	Common tern
Shelduck (W,P)	migration (P)	Arctic skua
Black guillemot (W)		
Guillemot (W)		Shorebirds in winter
Razorbill (W, P)		
Puffin (W)		
Roseate tern (R)		

trawlers, and settle rarely on the sea. Several species move out of the North Sea during the winter and are therefore not at risk in the area at this time.

There have been few records of wading birds being seriously affected by oil pollution. This may be because the birds are rarely in direct contact with the water. These species are therefore categorised as being at moderate risk in winter from oil pollution; it is likely that effects on the intertidal fauna on which these species feed would have greater effects on local populations. In summer, those wading birds that breed in saltmarshes are at higher risk. In a few cases, a large proportion of the world population of some species may be present in a small area during migration; these concentrations are categorised also as being at higher risk.

Oil pollution can take many forms. Many of the consequences depend on the type of oil involved. Light oils, such as many of the North Sea crudes, have a high evaporation rate and may have many components that will dissolve in the water column and disperse naturally. Only a small proportion of the spill may remain on the water-surface after one or two days. Conversely, heavy fuel oils evaporate and break up extremely slowly, and these will thus remain on the

Shelduck

surface and be a danger to birds for a much longer period. Stormy weather accelerates break-up of the oil, but may also cause emulsions with water, which take longer to disperse.

The size and timing of oil spills may be of less importance than the location of the pollution. The large blow-out on the Ekofisk field in the central North Sea in April 1977, when about 9000 tonnes of crude oil were spilt, caused very few seabird casualties. A small spill of only 550 litres of fuel oil in the Firth of Forth in 1978 led to the deaths of over 1400 birds.

The maps

In order to portray information on areas of importance, one map has been compiled for each month of the year to show known areas of the North Sea holding concentrations of birds at very high, high or moderate vulnerability to pollution. A page of text accompanies each map, highlighting major movements of birds relevant to the map and describing important concentrations of birds. The maps are in sequence from the breeding season onwards.

The maps have been compiled from two main sources. For inshore and estuarine areas, the most recent available reports and sources have been analysed to determine the location of important concentrations of birds. For British coasts, the main sources are the Birds of Estuaries Enquiry (BOEE), organised by the British Trust for Ornithology (BTO) and sponsored also by NCC and the Royal Society for the Protection of Birds (RSPB); the Winter Shorebird Count, a survey of non-estuarine shores jointly run by the BOEE and the Wader Study Group; and the National Wildfowl Counts operated by the Wildfowl Trust under contract with NCC. The locations of important bird colonies come partly from the Seabird Colony Register (currently unpublished) being compiled by the Seabird Group and the NCC for the British coast and partly from various continental sources.

Information for the offshore area is derived from an analysis of work carried out by the Seabirds at Sea Team between 1979 and 1986. This work, described in full by Tasker et al. (1987), aimed to establish which areas of the North Sea were important to seabirds when away from their breeding colonies. Much of the work of the team consisted of counting seabirds seen from ships, using a standardised method. This enabled comparisons between areas and assessments of the most important areas to be made. In order to compile each of the maps in this document, the monthly distribution maps for all seabirds were analysed and the importance of each area of the North Sea to every species was categorised as high, medium or low. Much of the information on the Moray Firth derives from a project carried out by the RSPB under contract to Britoil plc. In general, most of the North Sea has been surveyed for seabirds, but some areas remain to be checked. These are marked on the individual monthly maps. Coverage of the western North Sea is, in general, better than that for the eastern side. Some potentially important areas, especially off Denmark and the Netherlands, remain to be examined.

The maps were then drawn, using a combination of this categorisation and the species vulnerability ratings. An area of high importance to a species of very high vulnerability was graded most at risk from pollution and given the darkest shading. An area of medium importance to a species of very high vulnerability or of high importance to a species of high vulnerability was given a lighter shade. An area of low importance to a highly vulnerable species, medium importance to a species of high vulnerability or high importance to a species of moderate vulnerability was shaded with a light shade. Other areas held relatively few birds or have not been surveyed adequately. These two categories were also separated for mapping.

Mapping limitations

Birds are capable of rapid movement from one site to another. This adds to the difficulties of compiling maps of bird distribution. At some times of year, seabirds are constrained by the need to be close to the breeding site, while at other times their distribution may be controlled more by the location of food resources. For inshore and coastal species, these food resources are relatively predictable and static, but there may be large year-to-year differences in the amount and distribution of spat-settlement of bivalve molluscs as well as weather considerations which affect the availability of prey animals to some birds. The food resources of the offshore species vary in their precise location and abundance between years; in many

cases the reasons for this variation are unknown.

During the first seven years (1979—1986) of the Seabirds at Sea project, certain patterns became clear. One example is the post-breeding movement of guillemots and razorbills. The birds that breed on Shetland leave the waters of that archipelago soon after the chicks fledge from the cliffs. The birds then move southwards and eastwards, until in August they are found in large flocks off the east coast of Scotland or north-east coast of England. The precise location of these concentrations has varied between years. In 1980 and 1981 very large numbers were found off north-east England, in 1984 the largest numbers were present off the Firth of Forth and Grampian, while in 1985 the concentrations were further north off Grampian and in the entrance to the Moray Firth. In all years there was a large-scale movement away from Shetland waters.

The maps are therefore drawn to encompass all areas where concentrations have been known to occur within the 1980s. Owing to potential changes in distribution, these maps should not be taken as definitive, but rather should act as a warning of the potential consequences of pollution within an area.

It should be noted that concentrations of birds on areas of fresh or brackish water that are easy to protect from oil originating in the open North Sea are not plotted (e.g. Limfjord, Jutland and much of the Delta region of the Netherlands).

Use of the maps

This document has been designed for those concerned with the control of oil pollution. It presents a convenient summary of information on the birdlife of the North Sea in order that decisions which might affect this internationally important resource can more easily be made.

In the event of an oil pollution incident, the importance to birds of the affected area may be rapidly assessed by consulting the relevant monthly map(s). Oil spills from platforms on the United Kingdom continental shelf should be reported to NCC in accordance with Department of Energy's Continental

Shelf Operations Notice no. 7.

Immediate action is recommended to control spills in the areas of greatest and secondary importance. We recommend that any oil pollution in these areas be contained, dispersed or removed as soon as possible. The preferred method of clean-up will vary between incidents, but in principle physical removal of as much oil as possible is desirable. Spills in other areas should be treated on a case-by-case basis, and surveys should be conducted in the area of the spill to locate any vulnerable concentrations of birds.

It is anticipated that the oil spill contingency plans of the offshore operators for new operations will reflect these latest data, and those for existing operations will be revised to include them.

The maps may also be used to determine the timing of potentially risky operations. If such an operation is planned, reference to the area on each of the monthly maps should reveal the period of least vulnerability.

Research continues in the North Sea; this will undoubtedly refine and increase knowledge, particularly in those offshore areas not surveyed before this document was prepared. Up-to-date information on the birds of the North Sea and areas west of Britain, and their vulnerability to

pollution, may be obtained from the authors at:

Seabirds at Sea Team,
Ornithology Branch,
Nature Conservancy Council,
17 Rubislaw Terrace,
Aberdeen,
AB1 1XE
Tel. 0224 642863
(first point of contact)
or
Ornithology Branch,
Nature Conservancy Council,
Northminster House,
Peterborough,
PE1 1UA
Tel. 0733 40345
(in case of difficulty)

Common scoter

June

Inshore and coastal birds

June is the peak of the breeding season, and most of the migrant birds that spend the winter on the coasts of the North Sea or pass through on migration have returned to their breeding grounds. For most species these grounds are far to the north of the North Sea in arctic and cold temperate areas from northern Canada to Siberia. Eiders are the only seaduck that breed in any numbers around the North Sea. The main breeding colonies are in Shetland, Orkney, Grampian, Firth of Forth, Farne Islands, Dutch Wadden Sea, and Amrum in the German Wadden Sea. They are present in lower numbers along much of the rest of the Scottish, Danish and Norwegian coasts. Immature male common scoter start to arrive in the Danish Wadden Sea to moult later in the month.

Shags and cormorants remain inshore throughout the year; the majority of shags (19 800 pairs, which represent over 10% of the world population) in the North Sea breed on the rocky coasts of the north-west, with relatively few along the Norwegian coast. Most cormorants (2200 pairs) are also found in this area.

Terns breed along most coasts of the North Sea, especially on low shores, saltmarshes and islands. Most feed close inshore, but some forage up to 20km off the coast of Denmark. The entire North Sea population (36 pairs) of the endangered roseate tern breeds in north-eastern England and south-eastern Scotland. The largest numbers of little terns breed on the coasts of the southern North Sea; maximum numbers are on British coasts south of the Humber and continental coasts south of the Skagerrak (total North Sea population 2300 pairs). Sandwich terns are more common (30 500 pairs) than little terns and are also concentrated in the southern North Sea. Arctic terns (74 700 pairs) and common terns (61 500 pairs) breed on most coasts of the North Sea. About three-quarters of the arctic terns are found in Shetland and Orkney, while about a half of the common tern population of the North Sea is found in the Skagerrak. A third of common terns in the North Sea nest in the Wadden Sea.

There are few wading birds on the estuaries at this time of year, in comparison to the vast numbers that use these areas outside the breeding season. Substantial proportions of the small north-west European populations of spoonbill, redshank and ringed plover breed on the shores of the North Sea. These species are under threat in parts of their ranges. It is thus particularly necessary that these small populations should be safeguarded; important areas include the Wadden Sea and the Wash.

Offshore seabirds

The main breeding areas for the offshore seabirds in the North Sea are in the north-west. Most of them breed on cliffs or on rocky islands safe from mammalian ground-predators. The majority of this habitat occurs in the northern North Sea, with the notable exceptions of Helgoland and east Yorkshire. Breeding habitat is not the only requirement; there appears to be much suitable coastline in Norway, but this area holds relatively few breeding seabirds. Human exploitation in Norway may have reduced numbers in the past, but it is more likely that the present reason for this distribution is a lack of suitable food off the Norwegian coast.

About 680 000 guillemots have been counted in colonies (generally on cliff-ledges) on North Sea coasts. It is difficult to relate this figure to numbers of breeding pairs, but it is likely that these amount to about 500 000. The majority of these breed in Orkney, Shetland and the Moray Firth, with important concentrations further south on the east coast of Scotland and north-east coast of England. There are also colonies on Helgoland and Utsire. Recent surveys have shown that most breeding guillemots in the North Sea do not feed further than 30 km from their breeding sites in June. At the end of the month, guillemot chicks start to leave their colonies and disperse into the northern North Sea—see July. Some 73 000 individual razorbills (also mainly cliff-nesting) have been counted in North Sea colonies; this figure represents over 10% of the world population. These have a very similar distribution to that of guillemots. Breeding razorbills appear to feed closer inshore than do guillemots. Puffins breed in burrows in soil or in crevices on cliffs. 45% of the North Sea puffin population (about 225 000 individuals) breed in Shetland, with other large colonies on the Isle of May (Firth of Forth), on the Farne Islands and in Orkney. About half of the black guillemot population in the North Sea (23 700 individuals) breeds in Shetland, with the majority of the remainder in Orkney. Black guillemots feed close inshore, and most birds stay near their breeding sites throughout the year. These sites are mainly on islets, but also on cliffs away from ground-predators.

Gannets nest in a small number of cliff and islet colonies in Shetland and on Bass Rock (Firth of Forth); there is also a small colony on Flamborough Head (Yorkshire). Numbers in Shetland (four sites) are about the same as numbers on the Bass Rock (21 600 nests). Numbers of gannets breeding in the North Sea represent about 17% of the world population. During June, most adult gannets forage within 120 km of their breeding sites; many stay very much closer.

Kittiwakes also breed mainly on cliffs around the north-western North Sea. 415 400 nests have been counted and over a quarter of them in Orkney. Kittiwakes forage in much the same areas as guillemots but, unlike the auks—guillemot, razorbill and puffin—which can dive to great depths, they can feed only on fish that are near the surface.

The majority of the North Sea populations of great and arctic skuas breed in Orkney and Shetland. These birds feed close to the breeding sites, often within sight of the colonies. The total North Sea populations are 7300 and 3200 pairs respectively. The breeding great skuas represent over half of the world population. Gulls nest in large numbers on nearly all coasts of the North Sea. However, in the western North Sea it appears that most feed on land or on inshore habitats at this time of year and are therefore less at risk than at other times. The marine habitats off southern Norway and off the entrance of Skagerrak are more heavily used by gulls (mainly lesser black-backed) than other marine areas. Most parts of the

Arctic skuas

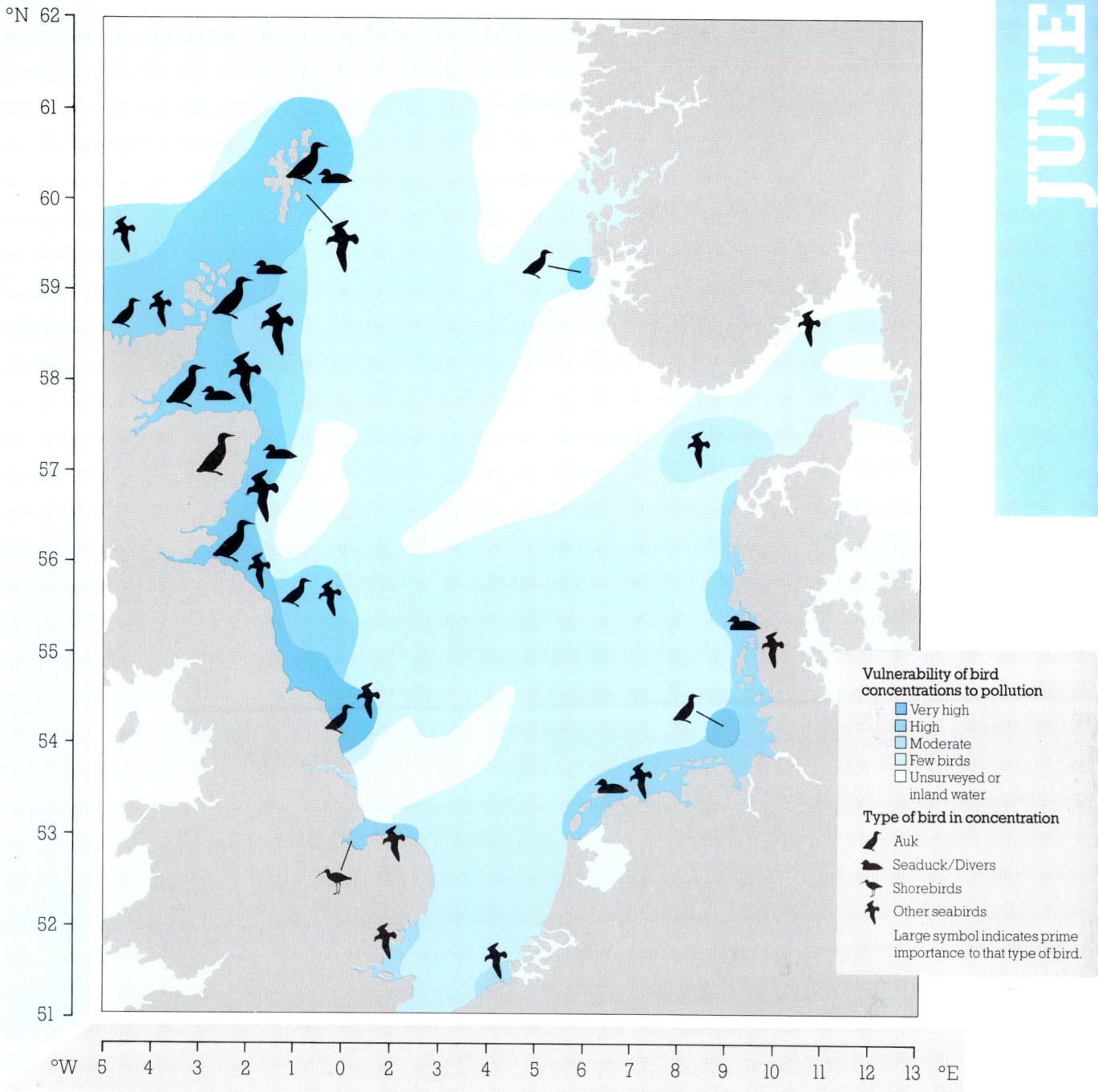

°N

62
61
60
59
58
57
56
55
54
53
52
51

°W 5 4 3 2 1 0 2 3 4 5 6 7 8 9 10 11 12 13 °E

Vulnerability of bird concentrations to pollution

- Very high
- High
- Moderate
- Few birds
- Unsurveyed or inland water

Type of bird in concentration

- Auk
- Seaduck/Divers
- Shorebirds
- Other seabirds

Large symbol indicates prime importance to that type of bird.

central North Sea are relatively empty of birds during June. Surveys have not been conducted off south-west Norway, off the Wash and Humber, nor to the north and north-west of Shetland. However, it is unlikely that many birds will be in these areas.

July

Inshore and coastal birds

For many species, the nesting season ends in late June or early July. At this time, adult and juvenile birds of several species may start to move south towards, or as far as, their wintering areas. Other species may move to moulting sites; often these are different from wintering areas. As some auks and ducks become flightless during this moult, and the flight of other species may be impaired, the moulting sites have to be safe from ground-predators.

One of the best known of these moult sites is that of shelduck. The majority of the north-west European population of about 100 000 birds moults on the Grosser Knechtsand in the Helgoland Bight. Numbers in the area start to increase in June and reach a peak in August; with some moulting birds still present in October. These birds are flightless and remain on the water over high tide periods, thus being vulnerable to any surface pollution. Smaller concentrations of shelducks occur on the Firth of Forth, the Humber and the Wash.

Common scoter also undertake a spectacular moult migration. Several hundred thousand birds from the populations breeding east of the Baltic migrate to moulting areas around the North Sea. The largest of these moulting flocks is in the Danish part of the Wadden Sea (150 000), but smaller flocks occur in other parts of the Wadden Sea, in the Jammerbugt and off Grampian, north-eastern England and the outer Thames estuary. Similar areas are used by moulting eider; 80 000 birds are estimated to moult off the west coast of Denmark and similar numbers have been found in the Dutch sector of the Wadden Sea. A large flock of moulting red-breasted mergansers occurs off the west coast of Denmark. The area off Grampian also supports a large flock of moulting eider. Further north, moult flocks occur in Scapa Flow and Wyre Sound, in Orkney and off various parts of Shetland at this time. The Firth of Forth is also important for eider.

After their breeding seasons, several species of wading birds move on to the estuaries and mudflats of the North Sea. All sectors of the Wadden Sea become internationally important, especially for knot, curlew, spotted redshank, redshank, greenshank and turnstone.

On the western side of the North Sea, large numbers of waders move to the Wash; the area is internationally important for grey plover, knot, sanderling, bar-tailed godwit, curlew and redshank. Numbers of curlew at Foulness also exceed the international levels of importance, while three other East Anglian estuaries, the Stour/Orwell, Blackwater and Leigh, hold internationally important numbers of redshank.

Offshore seabirds

At the end of June and during July, large numbers of seabirds leave their colonies and disperse out to sea. The most important of these movements are those of the larger auks. Young guillemots and razorbills leave their colonies before they can fly, at about one third of their adult weight. These young birds are accompanied to sea by the male parent and are fed and reared away from the colony. At the same time, immature and non-breeding birds also leave the vicinity of the colonies and disperse out to sea. Breeding females remain near their breeding sites for up to two weeks after the departure of the chicks. During the latter part of the month, all of the fully-grown birds lose the ability to fly due to the moult of their primary flight-feathers.

The large auks are thus particularly susceptible to oil pollution at this time and, because of their widespread dispersion, many areas of the North Sea hold vulnerable populations. The area of the Shetland Basin oilfields holds more birds than at any other time of year; flocks are present in the Norwegian sector and over some of the banks in the central North Sea. Large numbers are present off the Moray Firth and Grampian—see August.

Attendance at the colonies by breeding puffins, kittiwakes and gannets continues for much longer than that of the large auks. Young kittiwakes and puffins start to leave their nests late in the month. The areas near the main colonies of these species (Firth of Forth to Shetland) remain important for the whole month. There is some indication that the feeding range of gannets around Shetland

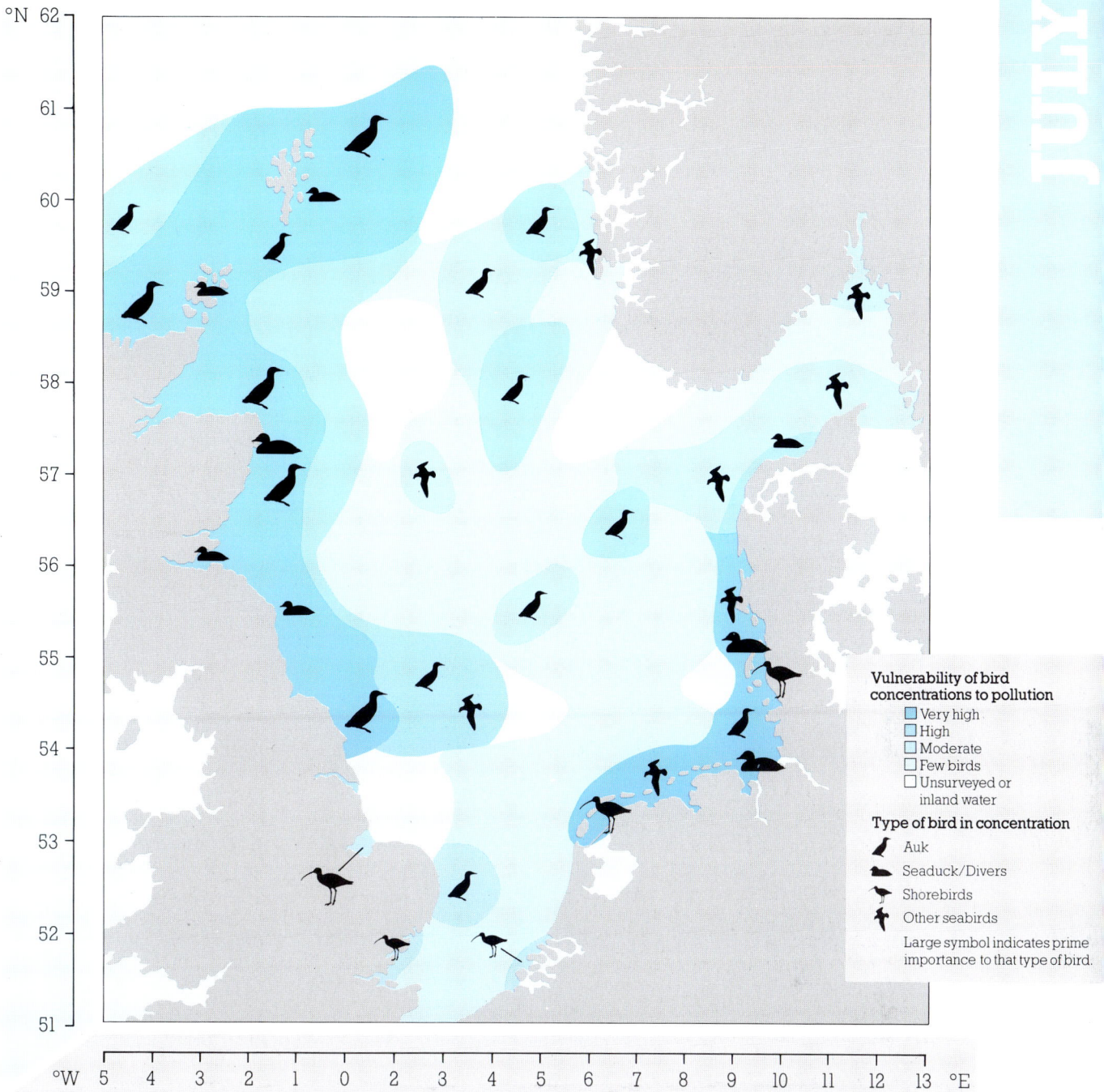

Vulnerability of bird
concentrations to pollution
- Very high
- High
- Moderate
- Few birds
- Unsurveyed or
  inland water

Type of bird in concentration

- Auk
- Seaduck/Divers
- Shorebirds
- Other seabirds

Large symbol indicates prime
importance to that type of bird.

expands during July, possibly associated with a change in diet. Large flocks (thousands) of non-breeding kittiwakes occur in the central and southern North Sea during July.

Numbers of great skuas present at their colonies reach a peak during July when many non-breeding birds are present. There is also an immigration of Manx shearwaters and storm petrels to the north-western part of the North Sea from areas west of Britain. Many of these also are non-breeding birds, as the breeding season for these species extends into August and most breeding birds are confined near their colonies in order to feed the chicks. Most terns finish breeding during the month, but the adults and juveniles remain close to their colonies (see June) for most of the month. The first migrant common gulls arrive in the North Sea from breeding grounds east of the Baltic; large numbers appear north of the Wadden Sea. Other gulls remain near their breeding sites.

There have been no surveys in the most northerly areas of the North Sea during July, including an area off western Norway that may prove important to auks. Smaller unsurveyed areas are off south-western Norway, in the central North Sea off Grampian and off the Wash. An area of poor coverage off the Wadden Sea may prove important for diving duck.

August

Inshore and coastal birds

August marks the start of the main influx of wading birds and ducks into the North Sea. Some of these birds remain in the area for the winter, but many move on southwards, in some cases after remaining for several weeks to moult or for a shorter time to feed and accumulate fat to fuel onward migration. Peak numbers for the year of several species of wader in the Wadden Sea are found during August. These include oystercatcher, ringed plover, grey plover, knot, dunlin, bar-tailed godwit, curlew, spotted redshank, redshank, greenshank and turnstone. The Dutch sector supports very large numbers of black-headed and common gulls at this time. The flocks of moulting shelduck, eider and common scoter remain in or off the Wadden Sea at this time— see July.

A similar influx to that recorded on the east side of the North Sea occurs on the British coast. The Wash supports internationally important numbers of the same species as July with the addition of oystercatcher. Numbers of bar-tailed godwit reach an annual maximum on the Wash during August. Grey plover reach internationally important numbers on estuaries further south on the British coast—Blackwater, Dengie and the Medway. Virtually all of the larger estuaries in south-eastern England hold internationally important numbers of redshank at this time; in addition similarly high numbers are found on the Forth, Tay and Montrose Basin in eastern Scotland. The Stour has an internationally important flock of black-tailed godwit at this time, while Foulness, the Cromarty Firth and the Lindisfarne flats hold large populations of bar-tailed godwit.

Eider numbers in the Forth, off Grampian, in the Tay and around Lindisfarne remain high during August. The flock of common scoter off east Grampian reaches maximum numbers during the month.

The eastern coasts of the North Sea, but particularly those of Denmark, have large numbers of migrating terns. The area off Blavand alone holds up to 10 000 common terns.

Offshore seabirds

The most important single concentration of auks in the North Sea at any time of the year occurs off the east coast of Scotland and northern England during August. This concentration has been a subject of particular study during the Seabirds at Sea project. In all years of study almost all guillemots and razorbills left the immediate vicinity of Shetland shortly after the breeding season. Simultaneously, a large concentration of these birds has occurred further south. The exact location of the concentration varied during the years of study. In the early 1980s more birds were off north-eastern England, while in more recent years the main concentrations were further north.

In 1985, a survey of the North Sea south of Shetland, north of Newcastle and east of 0°S 15'W estimated that there were one million guillemots present. These were concentrated in the entrance to the Moray Firth and to the north-east of Grampian. Other smaller flocks were present east and south-east of the main colonies in Grampian and in the Firth of Forth. The large northern concentration was thought to contain about one-third of the birds from Shetland colonies. The remaining two-thirds moved east and south-east from Shetland, though their exact location has yet to be determined. Some birds have been found off western Norway and in the entrance to the Skagerrak.

Razorbills were found to behave in a different fashion. 145 000 birds were estimated in the area surveyed off eastern Britain, much the largest concentrations being close to the coast near the Pentland Firth. This concentration probably included almost all of the birds from Shetland colonies, as well as some from colonies to the north and west of Britain. Black guillemots moult at this time, and the birds often move to specific moult sites. Around Shetland, these sites are in sheltered inshore waters, often with considerable tidal flow.

Puffins do not moult until spring, and their behaviour is different from that of the other auks. Some birds are still breeding in the early part of the month. When the birds leave their colonies dispersion is very rapid. Puffins appear

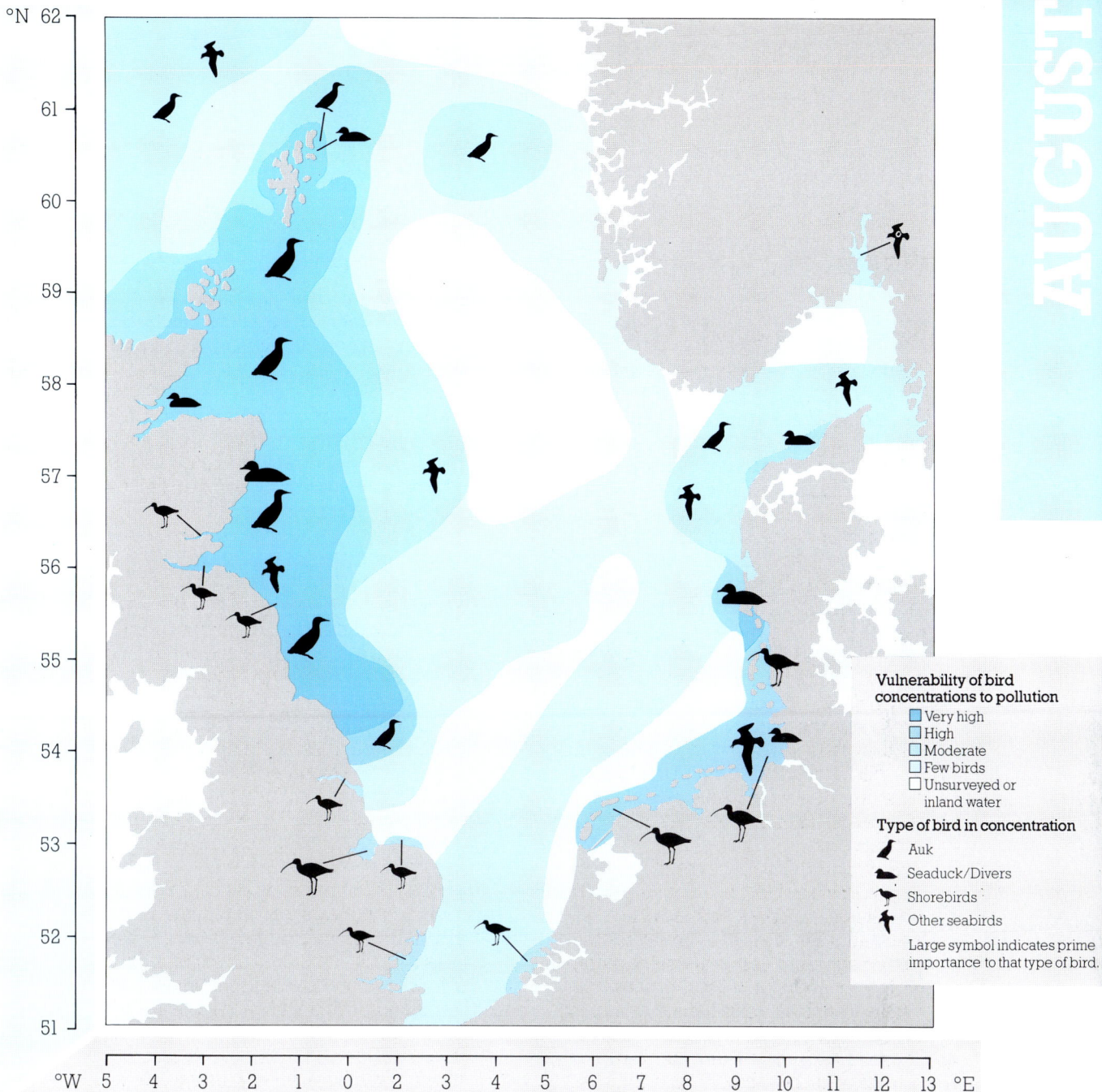

Vulnerability of bird
concentrations to pollution
- ☐ Very high
- ☐ High
- ☐ Moderate
- ☐ Few birds
- ☐ Unsurveyed or
  inland water

Type of bird in concentration

- Auk
- Seaduck/Divers
- Shorebirds
- Other seabirds

Large symbol indicates prime
importance to that type of bird.

to move northwards and westwards from Shetland, as well as to the south and east.

Kittiwakes and terns also leave Shetland waters in August and move to much the same areas as the larger auks off eastern Britain. Large movements of terns occur southward along the continental seaboard. Young gannets start to leave their colonies towards the end of the month. For a short period after leaving the colony, many of them are not capable of flying, and thus the areas close to colonies (Firth of Forth and Shetland) contain vulnerable populations of the birds.

Maximum numbers of petrels and shearwaters occur in the North Sea during August. Most of these birds do not breed in the North Sea but probably originate from populations breeding to the north and west of Britain. They concentrate mainly off the eastern coast

of Scotland. Manx shearwaters are found particularly off river mouths. Large numbers of lesser black-backed gulls occur in the Skagerrak and Southern Bight. There are relatively few gulls of other species present. One exception to this is the immigration of little gulls to a few sites within the North Sea. Flocks of this species occur off the Tay in Scotland.

There have been no surveys in a large area off southern Norway and in a band that runs north-east from Norfolk; coverage off Denmark and the Netherlands is patchy. The first of these areas may contain some auk concentrations.

September

Inshore and coastal birds

September is the peak month of usage of the North Sea estuaries. Over three million birds are present on the Wadden Sea, and many species are represented. Internationally important numbers of teal, mallard, pintail, oystercatcher, avocet, ringed plover, grey plover, knot, sanderling, dunlin, bar-tailed godwit, curlew, whimbrel, redshank and greenshank all occur on various parts of the Wadden Sea. In addition, large numbers of black-headed gulls are present on the Dutch and Schleswig-Holstein sections.

Very large numbers of waders and ducks use the estuaries on the British side of the North Sea also. The Wash is of greatest importance; 3% of the West European oystercatcher, 11% of grey plover and 3% of dunlin use the area. In addition, over 1% of knot, sanderling, curlew and redshank are present. Within the complex of estuaries in south-east England, several have internationally important numbers of grey plover and curlew, and most of them hold over 1% of the European redshank numbers. Further north, the Humber holds internationally important numbers of shelduck, grey plover, sanderling, curlew and redshank. The Lindisfarne flats hold internationally important numbers of wigeon (though these have declined in recent years), eider and bar-tailed godwit.

In Scotland, the Forth, the Tay and the areas off eastern Grampian and Golspie hold important numbers of eider. There is a large immigration of common scoter to the Moray and Dornoch Firths. These northern firths hold internationally important numbers of wigeon. The Firth of Forth is internationally important for bar-tailed godwit, curlew and redshank and has important numbers of great crested grebes. Internationally important numbers of bar-tailed godwit and redshank also occur on the Tay. Similar levels of redshank are present on the Eden, in the Montrose Basin and on the Cromarty Firth.

Large numbers of red-throated divers undergo wing-moult off the coasts of western Denmark, eastern Grampian and the southern Moray Firth during the month. This species breeds in Scandinavia, Greenland, Iceland and the Faroes, but the origin of the populations wintering in the North Sea is not known.

Offshore seabirds

During September, the distribution of auks spreads outward into the North Sea. The most important area for guillemots remains off the east coast of Scotland and north-east England, but the width of the area away from the coast is greater than in August. An area of primary importance for guillemots is present in the centre of the northern North Sea. Razorbills also congregate off eastern Scotland, with the largest concentrations in the Moray Firth and east of the Forth and Tay. There are very few in the southern North Sea at this time. Puffins, as in August, are further offshore than the other auks. The most important area is off the Firths of Forth and Tay. This area has been identified as being important for larval and young herring at this time. Herring is part of puffins' diet at other times of year and may be during this season also. It appears that the Orkney and Shetland populations of puffins move out of the North Sea and it is likely that the birds off eastern Scotland breed in the Firth of Forth and on the Farnes.

The area of primary importance for kittiwakes is also off the east coast of Britain, with the majority of the North Sea population off eastern Scotland. Gannets spread out into the North Sea during the month as their breeding season is completed. The most important area for Manx shearwaters is the inner Moray Firth, though the entrances to the Forth and Tay also have many birds. Sooty shearwaters do not venture as far south in large numbers as Manx shearwaters, but peak numbers are found in the north-western North Sea during September. The total number of sooty shearwaters arriving in the North Sea varies considerably each year. The nearest breeding locality for this species is on the Falkland Islands in the south Atlantic; the birds that arrive in the North Sea are likely to be non-breeders, as breeding birds are present at their colonies by late September.

Great skuas become very widespread in the North Sea in September as they leave their breeding

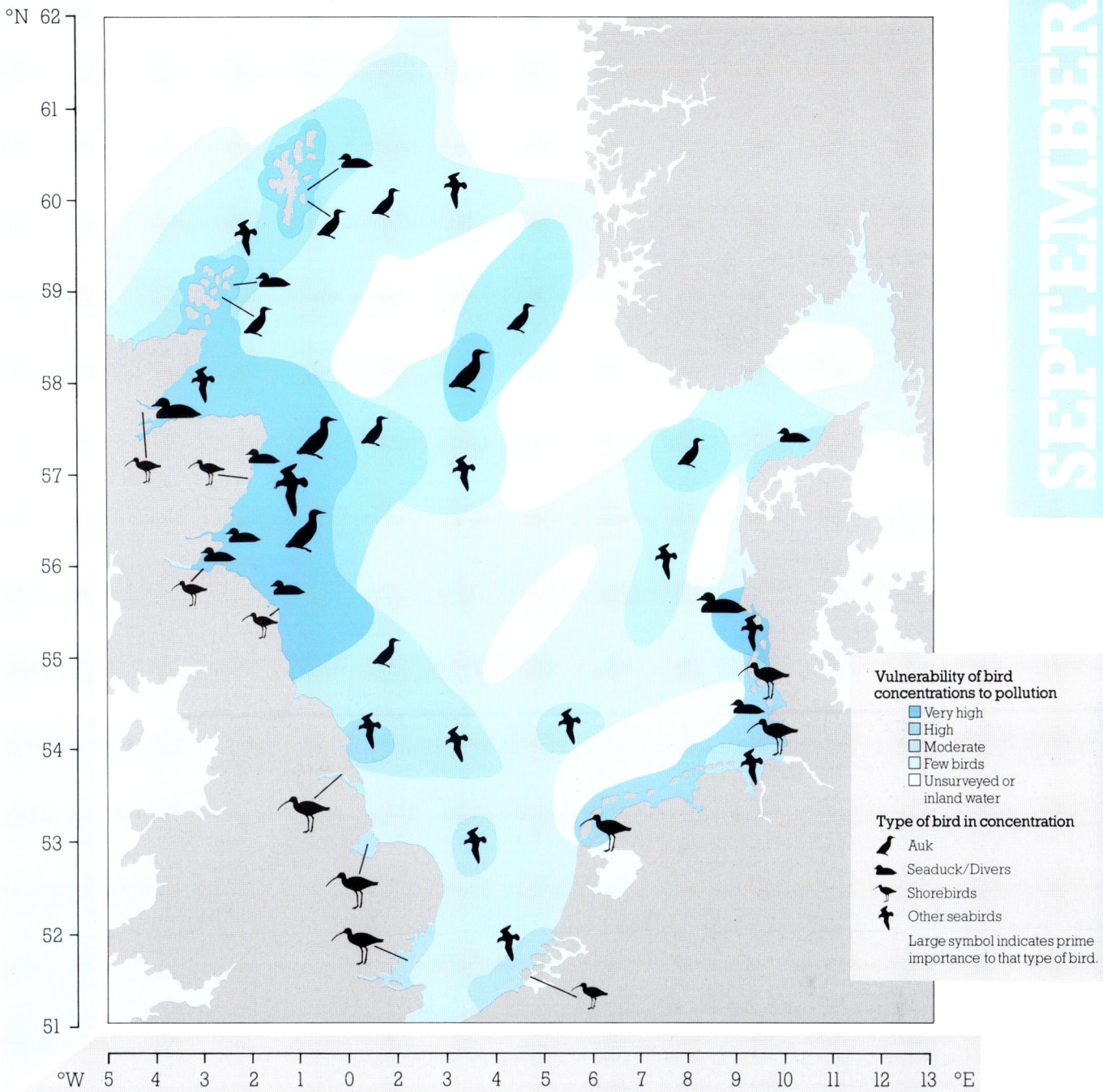

Vulnerability of bird concentrations to pollution
- Very high
- High
- Moderate
- Few birds
- Unsurveyed or inland water

Type of bird in concentration
- Auk
- Seaduck/Divers
- Shorebirds
- Other seabirds

Large symbol indicates prime importance to that type of bird.

sites and move south towards their wintering areas. Arctic skuas are scarce, as much of the population moves out of the North Sea during the month. Most lesser black-backed gulls have left the North Sea by the end of the month, and the only larger gulls at sea are great black-backed. These birds move across the North Sea from Norway during the month and are seen frequently around trawlers off the east coast of England. Storm petrels remain in reasonable numbers in the north near their breeding sites; most of the apparent non-breeders that were present off the east coast of Scotland in August have left the area. Fulmars are widespread and numerous across most of the northern and central North Sea.

An area off the Wadden Sea has not been examined in September nor have several large areas of southern and western Norway. Coverage of Danish and Dutch waters is patchy.

October

Inshore and coastal birds

There are fewer birds in the Wadden Sea in October than in September. This is due to migration from the area to the west and south-west. However, very large numbers of birds still remain, particularly ducks. There is immigration by brent geese, and more than 20% of the world population of the dark-bellied race of this goose is present off Denmark during the month. Brent geese normally roost on the water and hence would be at risk from oil pollution at this time. Wigeon, teal, mallard and pintail are all present in several areas in internationally important numbers. Shelduck remain in the area after their wing-moult, but spread out from their moulting sites in the German sector; thus the Dutch sector becomes more internationally important for this species. More than 100 000 common scoter are present off the Danish Wadden Sea. Very high numbers of oystercatcher, knot, sanderling, dunlin and curlew remain in the area. The large numbers of black-headed and common gulls that arrived in the area during

Curlew

August and September begin to disperse in October.

The Wash remains internationally important for oystercatcher, grey plover, sanderling, dunlin, bar-tailed godwit, curlew and redshank. On the Humber, four species exceed the 1% international levels—grey plover, knot, dunlin and redshank. Internationally important numbers of ringed plover, grey plover and redshank are present in various areas within the Thames estuary complex. Further north, the Firth of Forth holds large numbers of ringed plover, bar-tailed godwit and redshank.

Large numbers of red-throated divers are present in the Firths of Forth and Tay and off north-eastern Scotland during the month. Thousands are estimated to be in the area off the Danish Wadden Sea. These birds are in wing-moult and thus are more vulnerable than usual to any pollution. Influxes of common and velvet scoters and goldeneye occur during the month. Some 14 000 common scoter are found in the Dornoch/Moray Firth area; these birds have lower numbers of velvet scoters in association with them. Other smaller flocks of both species occur in the Forth along with an important flock of red-breasted mergansers and nationally important numbers of red-necked grebes. The area off the Tay estuary holds a large gathering of red-breasted mergansers at this time.

Offshore seabirds

There is a pronounced southward shift in the guillemot and razorbill populations in October. The area of the southern gas fields, off Norfolk and Lincolnshire, becomes important. The inshore band off Scotland and northern England still holds the largest numbers. During the month, guillemots return to some colonies on some mornings, presumably to defend nest sites. This habit occurs more often in the southern colonies (Isle of May and Grampian) than in the more northerly ones (Shetland). Razorbills return to the Isle of May on some mornings, but do not do so in the Moray Firth. Information on the bird populations of the central and eastern North Sea is poor, but some areas of importance to guillemots have been found. Razorbills are rare in the eastern North Sea. Puffin sightings are uncommon, but there are some indications that the offshore areas of the central North Sea hold most birds.

The centre of kittiwake distribution moves southwards also, and large numbers of birds are found off Yorkshire, as well as in areas further north (such as

62
61
60
59
58
57
56
55
54
53
52
51

Vulnerability of bird concentrations to pollution
- Very high
- High
- Moderate
- Few birds
- Unsurveyed or inland water

Type of bird in concentration
- Auk
- Seaduck/Divers
- Shorebirds
- Other seabirds

Large symbol indicates prime importance to that type of bird.

°W 5 4 3 2 1 0 2 3 4 5 6 7 8 9 10 11 12 13 °E

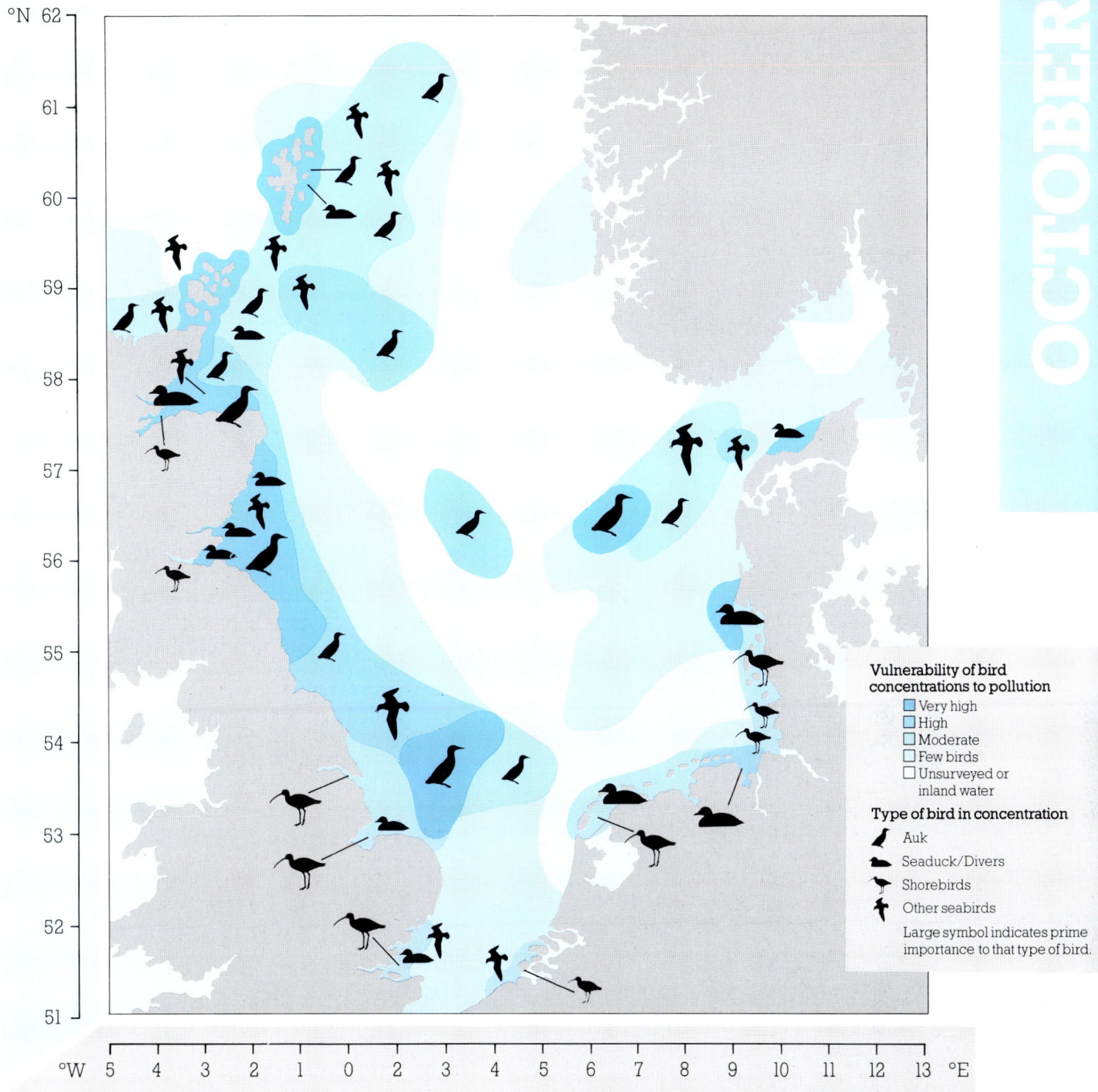

the Moray Firth). Large flocks have been noted on occasion off Holland also. Many adult and most immature gannets leave the North Sea during October. The only area where concentrations occur is off north-eastern England. Often these flocks are associated with fishing fleets. The few great skuas left in the southern parts of the North Sea are in this area; some also remain near the colonies in Orkney and Shetland. Most other summer visitors have left the North Sea by October. Sooty shearwaters are an exception; some remain in the Moray Firth. Little auks arrive in small numbers in the northern North Sea during the month from breeding grounds on islands in the Arctic Ocean.

Gulls are largely confined to the periphery of the North Sea. Some great black-backed gulls are in the area off north-eastern England frequented by several other species. These birds are associated with the fishing fleets in the area, as are many birds in the Moray Firth. Fulmars remain common throughout most of the northern North Sea.

In addition to the areas in the central and eastern North Sea noted above, much of the area to the north-west of Shetland has not been visited during October. The numbers of birds in the waters off the Wadden Sea are also unknown.

November

Inshore and coastal birds

The movement of waders from the Wadden Sea to the south and west continues through November. Many of the species which use the area only during migration or, in some cases, also for moulting, are present in low numbers. These species include ringed and grey plover, sanderling, bar-tailed godwit, spotted redshank and greenshank. Numbers of several other species may fall to low levels in November during periods of cold weather; these species include knot and oystercatcher.

Dark-bellied brent geese are still present in very large numbers on the Wadden Sea, mainly in the eastern sections. The flocks of light-bellied brent geese remain in the Danish Wadden Sea, but with some moving across the North Sea to Lindisfarne. The flocks of wigeon, teal, mallard and pintail that arrive in the Danish sector during September are still present in November. In the western Dutch sector, flocks of red-breasted mergansers and goosanders increase in size. Common scoter and red-throated divers are present off the Danish Wadden Sea in similar numbers to those recorded in October.

Many knot move westwards from the Wadden Sea and, in addition to the Humber, the Wash, the Tees, Lindisfarne and the Firth of Forth all assume international importance. Sanderling move westwards also; peak numbers occur on the Wash, with other internationally important numbers on the Humber and on Teesmouth. The sections of the Dutch delta area open to the North Sea become internationally important for sanderling and turnstone. Other estuaries with internationally important numbers of waders are little changed since October. Immigration by wading birds typically associated with non-estuarine shores occurs during the month. Internationally important flocks of turnstone appear on the coast of Shetland, Grampian and the Wash. Important sites for purple sandpipers include Shetland, Orkney, Grampian and the outer Firth of Forth. The flock of curlew in Orkney is also of importance; however many of the birds feed on inland sites.

Shelduck returning from their moult sites in the Wadden Sea form internationally important flocks on the Wash and at Teesmouth. The flock of eiders on the Tay has been recorded at over 12 000 during the month. A count of eiders in Scapa Flow, Orkney, has revealed 5400 during November. Goldeneye occur in some numbers in the Forth; other areas internationally important for this species include the Moray/Cromarty Firth, the Wash and the Colne. Both species of scoters have much the same distribution as in October. Long-tailed duck arrive in important numbers in the Moray Firth from breeding areas in northern parts of the USSR. The main feeding areas are along the south-western shore, but this species often feeds out of sight of land, so some important concentrations may remain undocumented. This duck also roosts offshore. Smaller concentrations occur elsewhere off the east coast of Scotland.

Offshore seabirds

The most important areas for guillemots and razorbills are off the eastern coast of Britain. The area off the south shore of the Moray Firth is important, as is an area to the south-east of Shetland. The east coast of Scotland holds relatively few birds in comparison to other times of year; an exception to this is the Firth of Forth and its approaches. The most extensive area of importance is off north-eastern England, stretching east to the Dogger Bank and south to the Outer Silver Pit. There is considerable immigration by guillemots to the Skagerrak during the month. A few razorbills are present in this area also. A concentration of guillemots and razorbills has been recorded off the Delta area of Holland. Of secondary importance are much of the remainder of the north-western North Sea, much of the Dogger Bank and around the gas fields off East Yorkshire. Lower densities of guillemots occur off northern Denmark during the month. There appears to be little change in puffin distribution between October and November, the main area within the North Sea being off Yorkshire and north-eastern England.

The main change in kittiwake distribution is the appearance of birds in substantial numbers in the Southern Bight. Flocks are found also around the

°N 62
61
60
59
58
57
56
55
54
53
52
51

°W 5 4 3 2 1 0 2 3 4 5 6 7 8 9 10 11 12 13 °E

Vulnerability of bird concentrations to pollution
- ☐ Very high
- ☐ High
- ☐ Moderate
- ☐ Few birds
- ☐ Unsurveyed or inland water

Type of bird in concentration
- Auk
- Seaduck/Divers
- Shorebirds
- Other seabirds

Large symbol indicates prime importance to that type of bird.

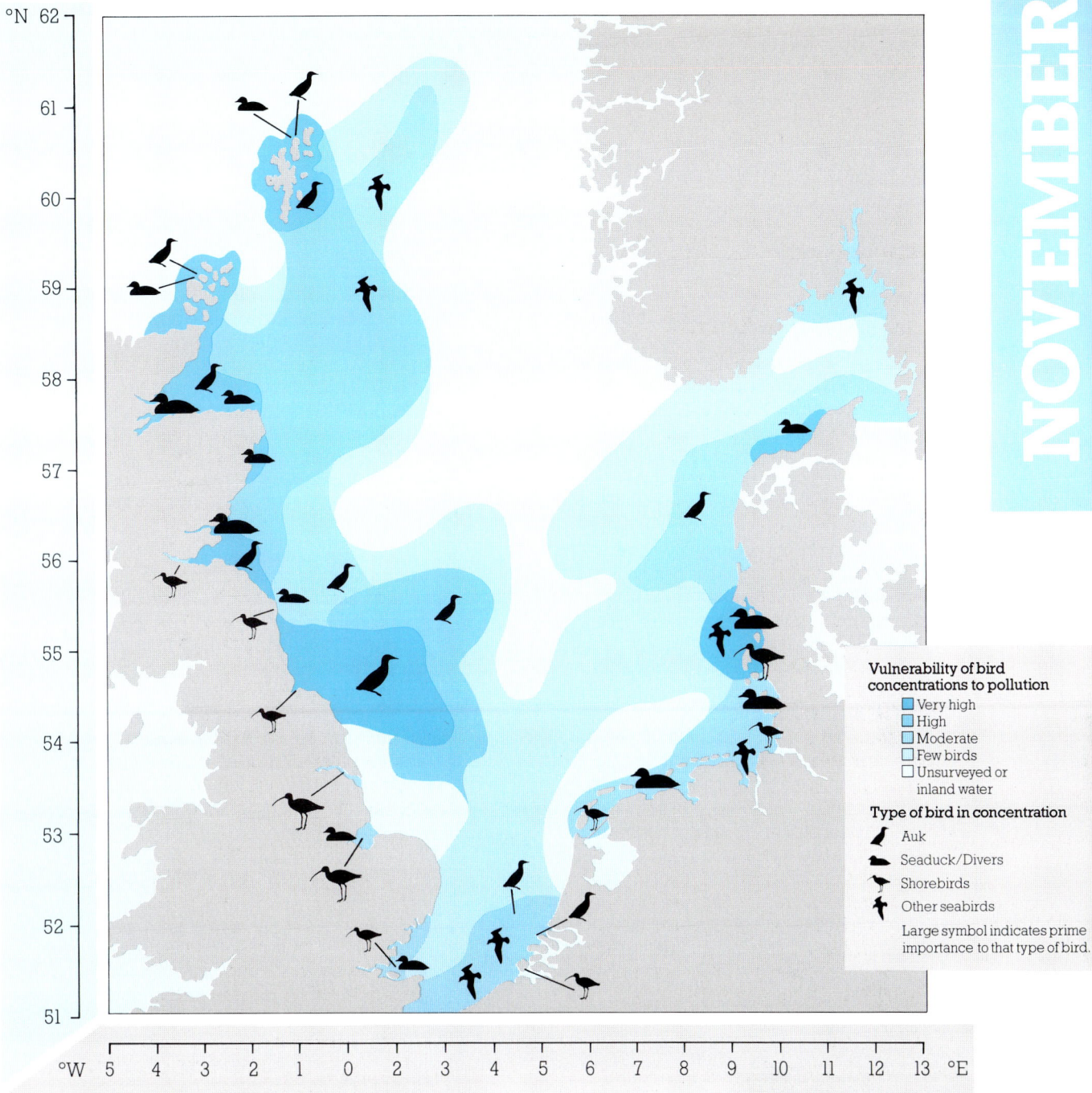

fishing fleets on the Fladden Ground. There are few gannets left in the North Sea in November; nearly all those present are adults.

In the northern North Sea several winter visitors become more common. One of the most obvious changes is the arrival of gulls in offshore waters. Herring gulls from Norway move south-westwards across the North Sea, and considerable numbers are present around trawlers in offshore areas such as the Fladden Ground. The Moray Firth remains an important offshore feeding area. Further south, the fishing fleets off north-eastern England attract many herring and great black-backed gulls. Some glaucous and Iceland gulls arrive from breeding grounds in Iceland, Greenland and northern Canada at the same time as these influxes. Common gulls become more abundant at sea in the Skagerrak.

An increasing proportion of darker-coloured fulmars indicates an influx of birds from the Arctic. Densities of fulmars are lower than in October, indicating some emigration from the North Sea by birds that bred in the area. Small numbers of little auks are also seen during the month; the most important area for this species appears to be off north-eastern England and eastern Scotland.

The area north and west of Shetland and most of the Norwegian sector of the northern North Sea have not been surveyed in November. Further south an area north of Holland and west of Denmark, and another off the Humber and Wash remain to be examined. Coverage of the central North Sea is poor.

DECEMBER

December

Inshore and coastal birds

Further emigration of waders from the Wadden Sea occurs during December; internationally important numbers of several species remain, but much depends on the severity of the winter. In warmer winters, many oystercatchers stay in the Dutch and Schleswig-Holstein sectors; in colder winters nearly all oystercatchers move westwards to Britain. Large numbers of waterfowl remain in the area, but they also are forced out during periods of freezing weather. The centre of their distribution moves west from off Denmark into the Dutch sector. Species present in high numbers in the Dutch sector include shelduck, teal, mallard, goosander and red-breasted merganser. Brent geese of both populations move westwards to Britain during December in most winters.

Further south, common scoter move into the area off the Dutch delta in internationally important numbers. These flocks remain in this area until March. Large numbers of scoter (both species) and divers remain in areas off the Danish Wadden Sea. Sanderling and

Brent geese

turnstone occur in internationally important numbers in this area also.

On British coasts, the most important areas for brent geese are in East Anglia,

Kent and Lindisfarne. The light-bellied geese at Lindisfarne feed intertidally, as do most of the dark-bellied further south, but some feed also inland. Most roost on estuaries at night. These waters may also act as refuges for freshwater ducks if their usual inland habitat becomes frozen. Several more estuaries become internationally important for shelduck during the month; these include the Medway, Blackwater, Colne, Hamford and Forth. The annual peak on the Forth (1500) occurs during the month. The Forth is also internationally important for eider, as are Lindisfarne, the Tay, the Ythan, Rosehearty (Grampian) and Golspie. The Moray Firth holds several internationally important flocks—long-tailed duck (in the same areas as in November), common and velvet scoters (annual peak of the latter species) and goosander and red-breasted merganser (in the Beauly Firth).

The Wash remains the most important estuary in the western North Sea for wading birds, with eight species at internationally important levels. The Forth has four species at this level and the Lindisfarne flats hold three. There are fewer estuaries with internationally important flocks of redshank than in November; these are Colne, Hamford, Stour, Orwell, the Wash, the Forth and the Cromarty Firth. Numbers and locations of other waders are little changed from November.

Offshore seabirds

The Southern Bight becomes important during December for guillemots. The movement into this area is probably associated with the sprats which shoal here at this time. There have been no surveys off northern Holland during December, but it is likely that this area is also important for guillemots, as sprat shoals are present here too. Large numbers of guillemots and razorbills are close to the coasts further north, the most important area being off the southern shore of the Moray Firth. This area has sprat shoals in some years, although recently there has been a decline in abundance. Some guillemots and razorbills may visit their nest sites on some mornings—see October. The principal area for puffins is the Outer Silver Pit, but they are present also in the central North Sea off north-east England and eastern Scotland.

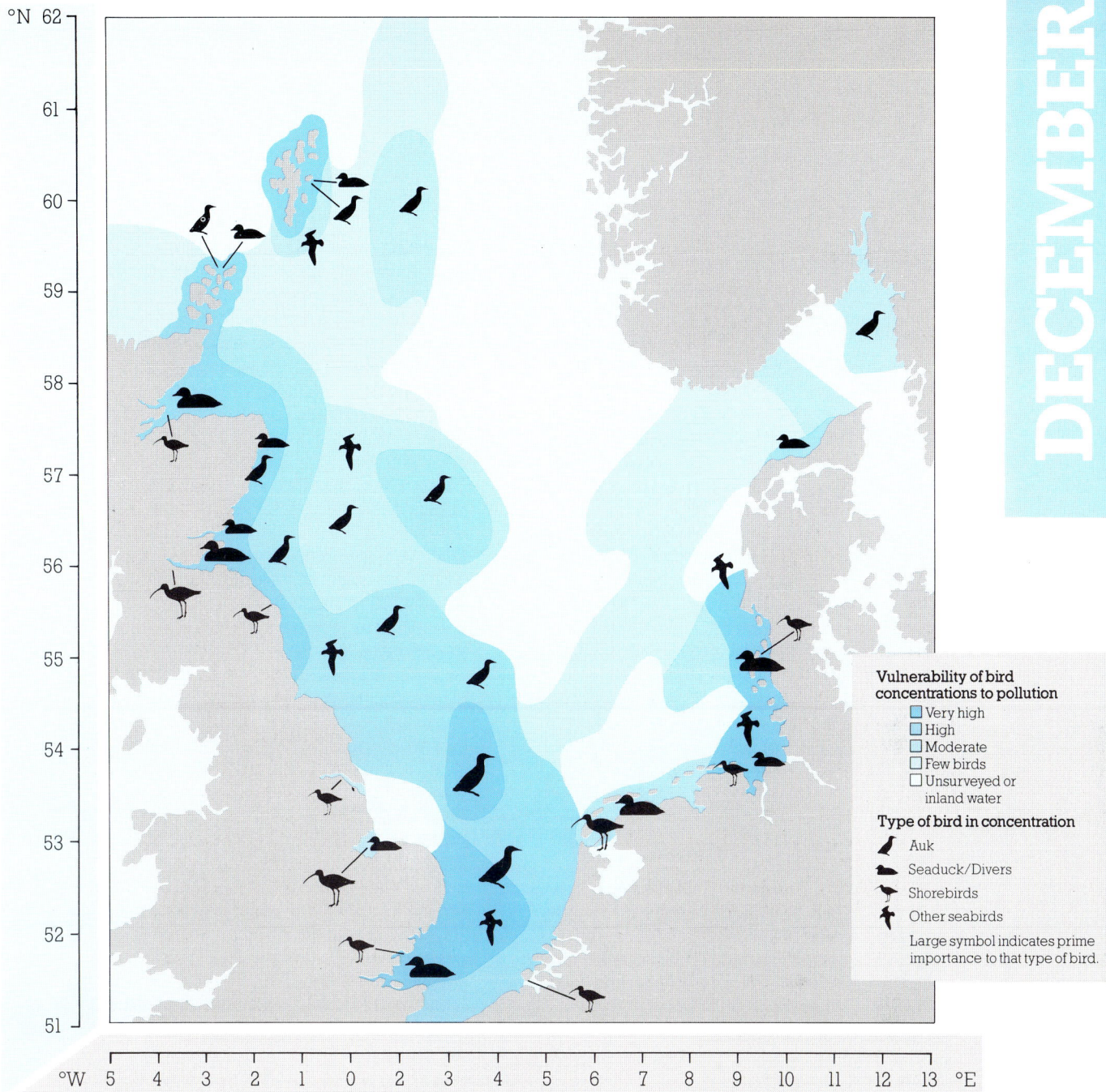

Vulnerability of bird concentrations to pollution
- Very high
- High
- Moderate
- Few birds
- Unsurveyed or inland water

Type of bird in concentration
- Auk
- Seaduck/Divers
- Shorebirds
- Other seabirds

Large symbol indicates prime importance to that type of bird.

The main areas holding kittiwakes are also in the southern North Sea and close to the north-east English and Scottish coasts. There are relatively few birds in the northern North Sea. Very few gannets occur anywhere in the North Sea. Little auks are present in considerable numbers in the western North Sea, with highest numbers over the Dogger Bank and inshore towards Yorkshire. Little auks are rare in the eastern North Sea during December.

There are still large numbers of gulls at sea. Common gulls have a coastal distribution and are mostly in the southern and eastern North Sea. Herring gulls are commonest in the western half of the North Sea, while great black-backed gulls have a more inshore distribution off the British coast. Many of these birds feeding at sea depend on trawler waste. At weekends and during

holiday periods, when there are few fishing vessels at sea, large flocks may form on adjacent land or islands. Fulmars are commonest in the northern North Sea.

Survey of the North Sea during December has been poor, because of short days and bad weather. The Norwegian sector remains unsurveyed, as does the area north and west of Shetland. Areas north of Holland, off the Wash and Humber, off the Forth and east of the Dogger Bank remain unexamined.

27

January

Inshore and coastal birds

The distribution of inshore birds in the North Sea in January depends in part on the severity of the winter. More birds remain on the eastern side of the North Sea in mild winters than they do in colder winters, although the distribution of some species is little affected by year-to-year variation in weather. Within the Wadden Sea, more birds move southwards and westwards during the coldest parts of winter. Large-scale movements by great crested grebes, shelduck, scaup, red-breasted mergansers and eiders have all been recorded off continental coasts in times of severe weather. These movements often result in very large influxes of birds to England. Up to 20 000 great crested grebes may occur in severe weather in Dutch inshore waters, especially those off Zuid-Holland and Nord-Holland. The flock of red-breasted mergansers that gathers in the western Dutch Wadden Sea in winter reaches a peak in January, with 12 000 present; this represents about 15% of the total estimated west European population. An estimated 80 000 scaup may occur in the western Wadden Sea in severe winters. In mild winters, large flocks of shelduck, mallard and pintail remain in the Wadden Sea.

Among the waders, large numbers of oystercatcher, knot and curlew are present, all centred on the Dutch sector. If the winter is mild, some oystercatchers move back to their inland and coastal nesting sites during January.

The Thames Estuary and northern Wadden Sea are important for divers in January. In the latter area, divers are forced south by sea-ice in the coldest winters and become more abundant off the unfrozen estuaries of the German Wadden Sea. A minimum of 6000 red- and black-throated divers winter off the west coast of Jutland, with an additional 6000 off areas further south to Cap Gris Nez. Up to 1000 divers are present in the Thames Estuary and associated inshore waters in some winters.

The annual peak of shelduck on the Wash occurs in January. January counts exceeded 10% of the north-west European total. Winter peaks of shelduck occur also in the Thames Estuary complex, and further north Teesmouth and the Firth of Forth support internationally important flocks.

Large flocks of eider are present in several sites off eastern Scotland and north-eastern England. The common scoter flock in the Dornoch/Moray Firth area represents about 50% of the British population and 3% of the north-west European population; the peak of scoter numbers in January 1984 in the whole firth was 18 700. However, these numbers are low in comparison to the estimated 200 000 common scoter that occur off the Danish Wadden Sea every winter. Several sites in Britain including the Blackwater, the Colne, the Wash, the Tweed and the Forth, Cromarty and Moray Firths, support large flocks of goldeneye. These species are attracted to sewage outfalls which increase local food resources. When these outfalls are removed or cleaned the flocks disperse. This has happened, for example, in the Firth of Forth off Edinburgh, and at Peterhead, Grampian.

The long-tailed duck flock in the Moray Firth is the largest in the North Sea. Two internationally important offshore roost sites have been identified, one off Brora (about 7000 birds) and the other off Burghead (about 15 000 birds). Scapa Flow in Orkney holds a large flock of long-tailed duck in winter; large numbers of several other species are present also. Scapa Flow and Wyre/Rousay Sound in Orkney, and Yell Sound in Shetland, hold important flocks of great northern divers. Black guillemots are present throughout both of these northern island groups, but are concentrated in shallow, sheltered waters.

Offshore seabirds

Guillemots and razorbills remain abundant in the Moray Firth and close to the eastern coast of Scotland and northern England. There are guillemots throughout the southern North Sea, with particularly important flocks over the Outer Silver Pit. The western part of the Danish sector is important for razorbills also. Guillemots reappear in Shetland waters in January; a very few razorbills also return to the area in this month. Few puffins have been seen in January, but it is likely that these are in similar offshore

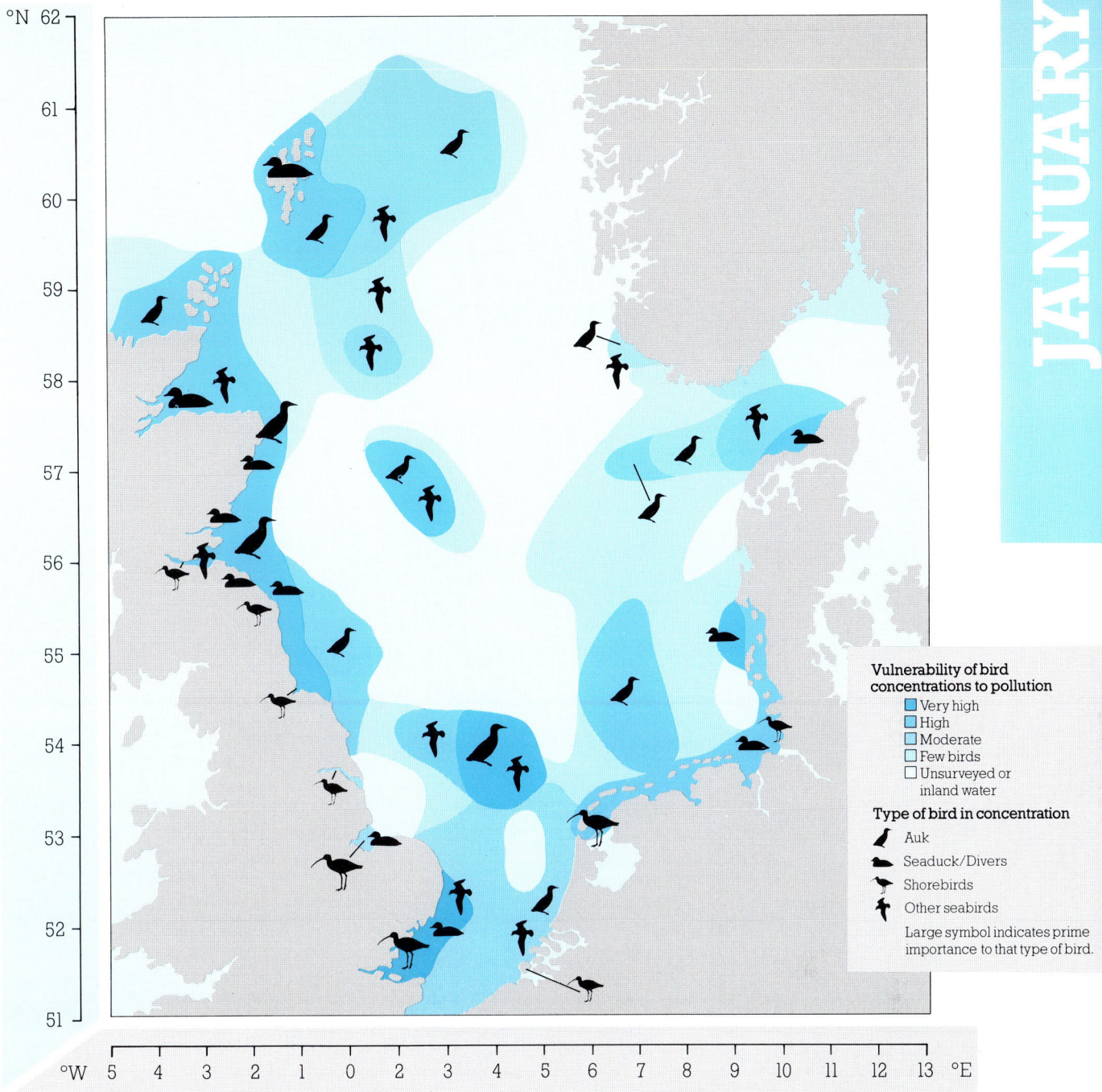

°N 62
61
60
59
58
57
56
55
54
53
52
51

°W 5 4 3 2 1 0 2 3 4 5 6 7 8 9 10 11 12 13 °E

JANUARY

Vulnerability of bird concentrations to pollution
- Very high
- High
- Moderate
- Few birds
- Unsurveyed or inland water

Type of bird in concentration
- Auk
- Seaduck/Divers
- Shorebirds
- Other seabirds

Large symbol indicates prime importance to that type of bird.

areas to those used in other winter months.

The entrance to the Skagerrak is important for kittiwakes in January, but the area east of Shetland and Orkney is the most important for them. Little auks occur in some numbers in the entrance to the Skagerrak during the month as well as being present off the east coast of Britain.

Common gulls occur in largest numbers in the Skagerrak, off the west coast of Denmark and in the Southern Bight. As in December, herring and great black-backed gulls are seen most frequently at sea in the Moray Firth and off the eastern coast of Britain. A few lesser black-backed and black-headed gulls are present offshore in the Southern Bight. Glaucous gulls reach an annual peak in the northern North Sea in January. Fulmars are present in most offshore areas of the northern and central North Sea. They are commonest off Shetland.

Survey effort offshore in the North Sea in January has been poor; thus it is possible that some important areas may remain to be discovered. The area to the north-west of Shetland has not been examined.

February

Inshore and coastal birds

Goosanders in the western Wadden Sea reach a peak in numbers during February and March at around 25% of the estimated west European population. Most of the birds are found near the outflow from the IJsselmeer. Another 12% of the population is present in the Danish Wadden Sea. These birds may move westwards if the winter is particularly cold. Other duck species are present in the Wadden Sea in lower numbers than in preceding months; many will have moved west to avoid the coldest part of the winter. Internationally important flocks of waders in the Wadden Sea include oystercatcher, knot and curlew; the most important areas for these species are in the Dutch sector. The waters off the Dutch delta and the Danish Wadden Sea remain internationally important for common scoter. In winters when ice covers the Kattegat and Baltic the North Sea becomes a refuge for more ducks and grebes. Areas such as the Jammerbugt become considerably more important than usual; holding, for example, up to 50 000 common scoter.

Kittiwake

Large numbers of shelduck remain on southern English estuaries; in addition to the Wash, the north Kent marshes, Medway, Blackwater and Stour all have internationally important flocks in February. Eiders remain in large numbers off eastern Scotland, with important flocks in the same locations as December. Scapa Flow in Orkney holds peak numbers of long-tailed ducks during the month, and large numbers remain in the Moray Firth. In addition, the Moray Firth area holds large numbers of common scoter, velvet scoter, goosander and red-breasted merganser (the latter two species on the Beauly Firth).

There is little change in the location of internationally important wader flocks between January and February, the Wash continuing to be the most important site in eastern Britain. Most of the estuaries in south-eastern England hold internationally important flocks of grey plover or redshank; Hamford Water is important for four species—ringed plover, grey plover, curlew and redshank. The Humber also gains in importance in comparison to January, with internationally important numbers of knot, sanderling, dunlin and redshank. Further north, the Forth holds peak numbers of bar-tailed godwit during the month, as well as having internationally important flocks of knot and redshank.

Offshore seabirds

Guillemots are distributed throughout much of the western North Sea, with main concentrations in the Moray Firth and Firth of Forth. Important numbers are present off most of the east coast of Scotland and in the Silver Pit. Substantial numbers are present in some years in the eastern English Channel and Southern Bight. Razorbills are present in much the same areas as guillemots, but, in contrast to January, a few birds return to Shetland waters in February. The Fisher Banks off northern Jutland are areas of secondary importance for both species. Puffins are present in largest numbers in the northern North Sea, to the east of Shetland, and are also distributed widely in most offshore areas.

Kittiwakes are found in largest numbers in the western North Sea, with particular concentrations in the Silver Pit area and off Orkney and Shetland. There is some return by adult gannets to the North Sea in February. They are found in much of the western North Sea; the area off north-eastern England is the most important. Little auks are commonest

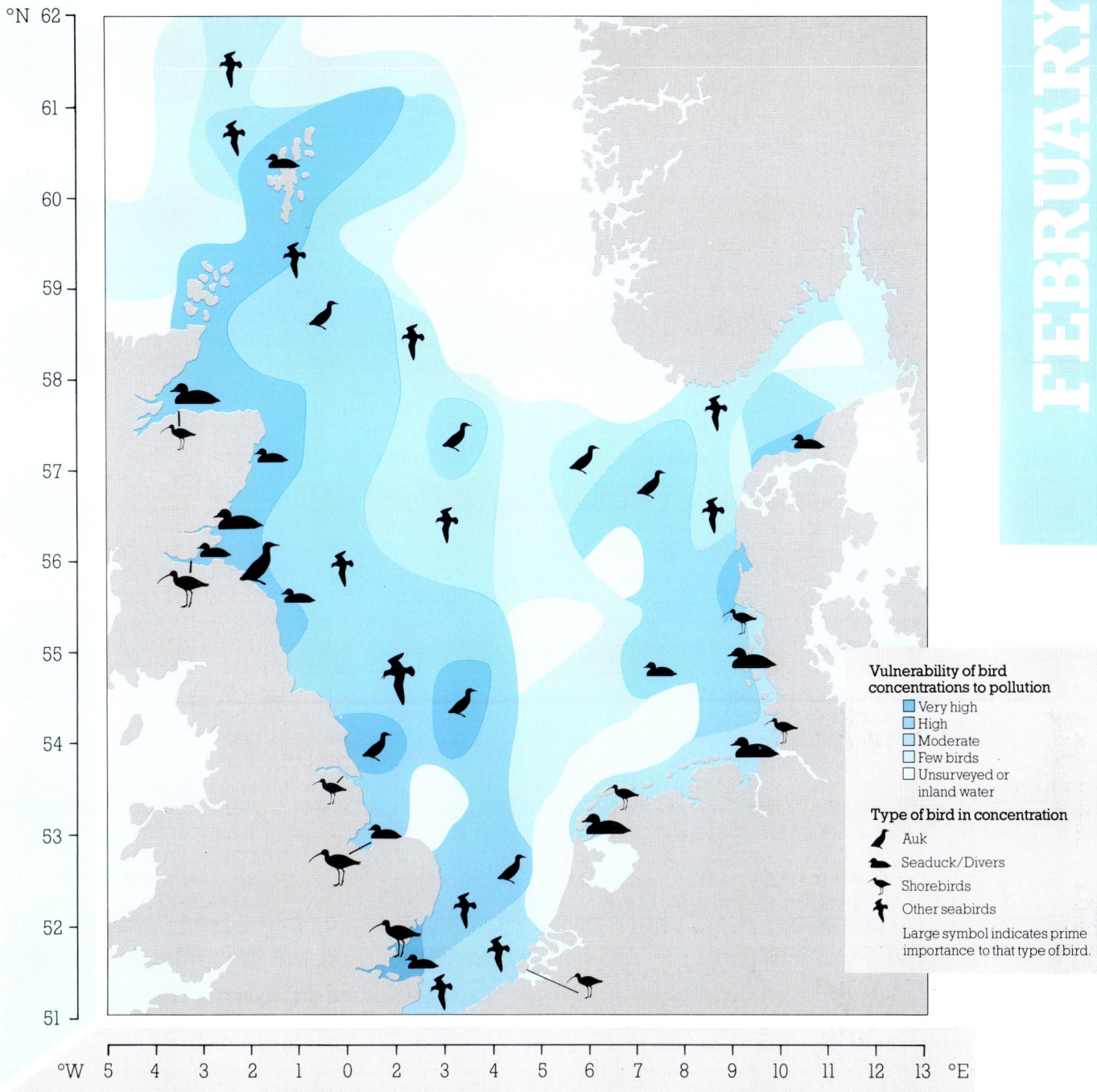

°N 62, 61, 60, 59, 58, 57, 56, 55, 54, 53, 52, 51

°W 5 4 3 2 1 0 2 3 4 5 6 7 8 9 10 11 12 13 °E

Vulnerability of bird concentrations to pollution
- Very high
- High
- Moderate
- Few birds
- Unsurveyed or inland water

Type of bird in concentration
- Auk
- Seaduck/Divers
- Shorebirds
- Other seabirds

Large symbol indicates prime importance to that type of bird.

over the Fisher Banks, and present in high numbers in other parts of the Skagerrak; moderate numbers are present in many other areas offshore in the western North Sea.

Herring and great black-backed gulls are commonest off eastern England, but are present also in other areas of the western North Sea. The distribution of both species is heavily influenced by the location of fishing fleets. Common gulls are most frequent off England south of Yorkshire and off southern Norway. Coverage of the area off the Wadden Sea is poor, but it is likely that this area is important for this species also. A few black-headed gulls are present in the Southern Bight. Fulmar distribution is very similar to that in January, with most near Shetland but some in much of the western North Sea.

Survey of the North Sea in February

has been better than in other winter months. The area off Norway remains to be surveyed, as do areas off the Wadden Sea, and parts of the southern half of the North Sea. Coverage off Denmark has been patchy.

March

Inshore and coastal birds

March marks the start of the return to breeding grounds by many species, and intertidal areas become less important in terms of absolute numbers than earlier in the winter, though the importance to passage populations increases. The western Wadden Sea remains internationally important for goosanders during March, when up to 25% of the west European population may be present. Another 12% of this species is found in the Danish sector. The Dutch sector holds over 5000 red-breasted mergansers. Up to 100 000 common scoter may be present off Dutch coasts, with the Delta, Zuid-Holland and Nord-Holland coasts being especially important. Curlews move through the Wadden Sea during the month and highest numbers in the year are noted in most sectors. Large numbers of dunlin are found in the Dutch and German sectors and annual peaks of sanderling are found on the sandy parts of the German sector.

Red-throated and black-throated divers move northwards in considerable numbers during the month, and the area off the west coast of Denmark becomes particularly important. Some of these birds may be found up to 80km from land in this area.

Numbers of wading birds decline on the British estuaries during March. The Wash is the most important area; internationally important numbers of oystercatcher, grey plover, knot, sanderling, dunlin, bar-tailed godwit and curlew are present. Grey plover, a species which nests in the high arctic, remains later in its winter quarters than some of the more temperate species. Internationally important numbers remain on such estuaries of south-east England as the Medway, Swale, Dengie, Hamford Water and Blackwater. Large numbers of bar-tailed godwit, another high arctic species, remain also; they prefer the larger estuaries, and internationally important numbers are found on the Foulness flats, at Lindisfarne and on the Firth of Forth in addition to those on the Wash. The Humber is internationally important for dunlin and knot.

A peak of 1700 shelduck occurs on the Eden during the month, with internationally important flocks on the Wash, Stour and Blackwater. A peak of great crested grebe occurs on the Blackwater also. Eiders move back towards their breeding areas; a peak of 3200 has been recorded on the Forth and about half this number on the Ythan.

Offshore seabirds

The majority of guillemots of breeding age have returned to the vicinity of their colonies in the north-west North Sea. Immature, non-breeding guillemots do not attend the colonies during this early part of the season. These birds may still be found in the eastern and southern parts of the North Sea; the Little Fisher Bank off northern Jutland is one area where many of them have been observed during the month. Immature and adult razorbills have a pattern of similar distribution to the guillemots, although proportionately fewer are found in the eastern North Sea. The Outer Silver Pit is important for this species.

Puffins return to the areas close to their colonies during the month. In the North Sea, the main colonies are in Shetland, the Firth of Forth and the Farne Islands, with substantial numbers on Orkney and Flamborough Head, Yorkshire. Kittiwakes are also found much closer to their colonies than in February. Many fewer are present in the southern North Sea; the main concentrations are in the north, off Orkney and Shetland. Gannets return to their breeding colonies during March, although some may have returned in February. These birds feed in the waters close to the colonies and thus the highest densities are found around Shetland and off the Firth of Forth.

Generally, great skuas are first observed in Shetland waters during the month, but some may be present also in the southern North Sea. Most migration to Shetland from the south must occur to the west of Britain. The main concentrations of little auks are found off southern (and probably western) Norway. Fulmars are present in highest density off their main breeding area (Shetland) during March, but some flocks are present also in the southern and central North Sea.

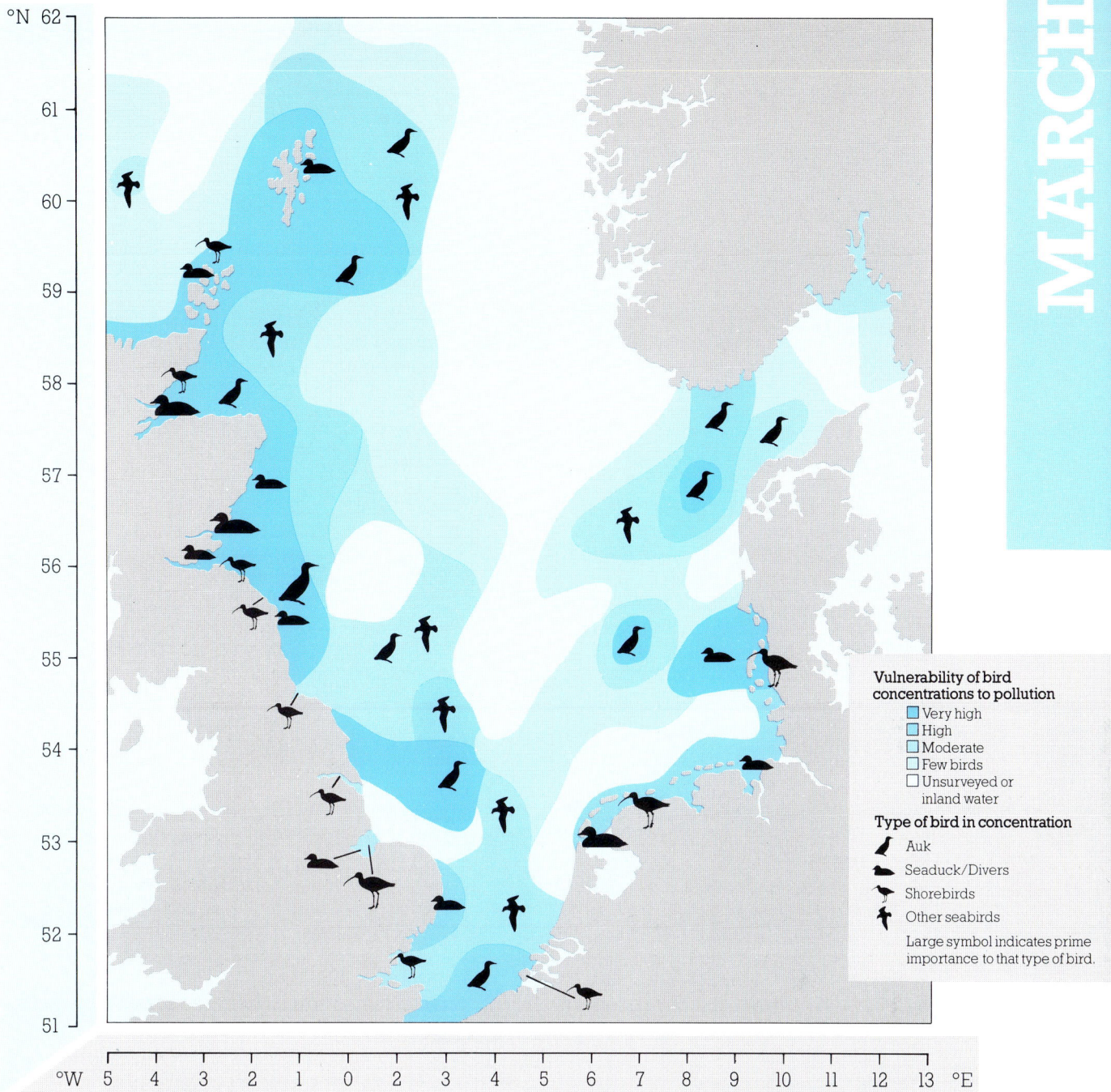

Vulnerability of bird concentrations to pollution

☐ Very high
☐ High
☐ Moderate
☐ Few birds
☐ Unsurveyed or inland water

Type of bird in concentration

Auk
Seaduck/Divers
Shorebirds
Other seabirds

Large symbol indicates prime importance to that type of bird.

Some eastwards migration by common gulls occurs during the month, and small flocks are observed at sea. This species becomes very common off Dutch coasts also. Herring and great black-backed gulls from Norway return north-eastwards; many fewer are seen off the east coast of England than earlier in the winter. Most of those that remain in this area are breeding birds. The Moray Firth and the area east of Shetland remain important for both species. A few lesser black-backed gulls return from their wintering quarters just south of the North Sea to their colonies on the eastern seaboard. In a similar fashion, little and black-headed gulls start to return to their colonies, to the east of the North Sea during the month; most of these birds migrate along the coasts of the eastern North Sea, though some are seen off British shores.

The area off Norway has not been surveyed at all in March, nor has a large part of the Dutch and German sectors off the Wadden Sea. A small area off the Farne Islands that may prove important to auks also needs to be surveyed. Coverage off western Denmark, and off eastern Scotland has been patchy.

April

Inshore and coastal birds

Many of the birds using the estuaries of the North Sea in April are on passage from southern wintering areas to their northern breeding grounds. Brent geese that have spent much of the winter on British and French coasts peak in numbers in the German sector of the Wadden Sea; most of the western European population is in the area at this time. The small light-bellied brent goose population is still present on its wintering areas until the end of the month. Brent geese feed on the mudflats, saltmarshes or grasslands by day, but roost afloat by night; thus they are vulnerable to any surface pollution of the sea. Dunlin are found in large numbers throughout the Wadden Sea. The Dutch sector supports large numbers of bar-tailed godwit, and about 5000 red-breasted mergansers remain in the area. The Dutch inshore sectors remain internationally important for common scoter (up to 100 000 birds), but these, as well as those off Denmark move northwards towards their breeding grounds during the month. The German sector has a large passage of spotted redshank. Grey plover pass through the area during the month, with peak numbers at the end of the month and in early May. Peak turnstone migration occurs on the Wadden Sea during the month.

British estuaries are less important in terms of absolute numbers of feeding waders between April and June than at other times of the year. However, counts of birds present at any one time will greatly underestimate the numbers of passage birds using a site. Even in terms of numbers counted, the Wash remains internationally important for dunlin, knot and curlew in April. The Humber is of international importance for dunlin. These east coast estuaries probably act as stop-over points for birds that wintered further south and west. They are also important for their numbers of breeding waders. Shelduck are present on the Wash in internationally important numbers. Eiders return to their breeding areas near the Tay, on Lindisfarne, on the Ythan and in Orkney and Shetland. Other concentrations of duck are found off Kent (common scoter), and in the inner Moray Firth (long-tailed duck and velvet scoter).

Black guillemots move close to their breeding areas during the early morning in order to display and secure a breeding site. The main concentrations are in Orkney, Shetland and Caithness.

Offshore seabirds

By the end of April some seabirds that breed around the North Sea will have started to lay eggs. Much of the seabird activity during the month is concerned with preparations for the breeding season. Many birds are establishing and defending territories. At the same time female birds will be feeding to gain in weight and improve body condition before egg-laying. Many seabirds are therefore close to their colonies, but some may be feeding further offshore than during the chick-feeding period. One example of this is found off Flamborough Head, where guillemots commute about 100 km from the colony in order to feed on large sandeel concentrations that occur at this time of year over the north-west part of the Dogger Bank. A similar situation is found to the south-east of Shetland. Low numbers of guillemots remain in the eastern and southern North Sea; these are probably all immature birds. Razorbills have a very similar distribution to that of guillemots. Puffins, are not, however, as close to the colonies as the two other auks and many are found in the centre of the North Sea to the east of Shetland.

Kittiwake distribution is very similar to that in March, with a wide distribution of birds in the western half of the North Sea, particularly in the north near the main breeding areas. Gannets are found in largest numbers near their colonies in the Firth of Forth and Shetland. Great skuas return to their breeding areas (Orkney and Shetland).

The north-eastwards migration by common gulls towards breeding grounds in eastern Europe continues across the North Sea during the month. The return of herring and great black-backed gulls to their breeding grounds in Scandinavia occurs mainly during March, but continues to a lesser extent in April. This is most evident in the northern North Sea, where flocks are frequently

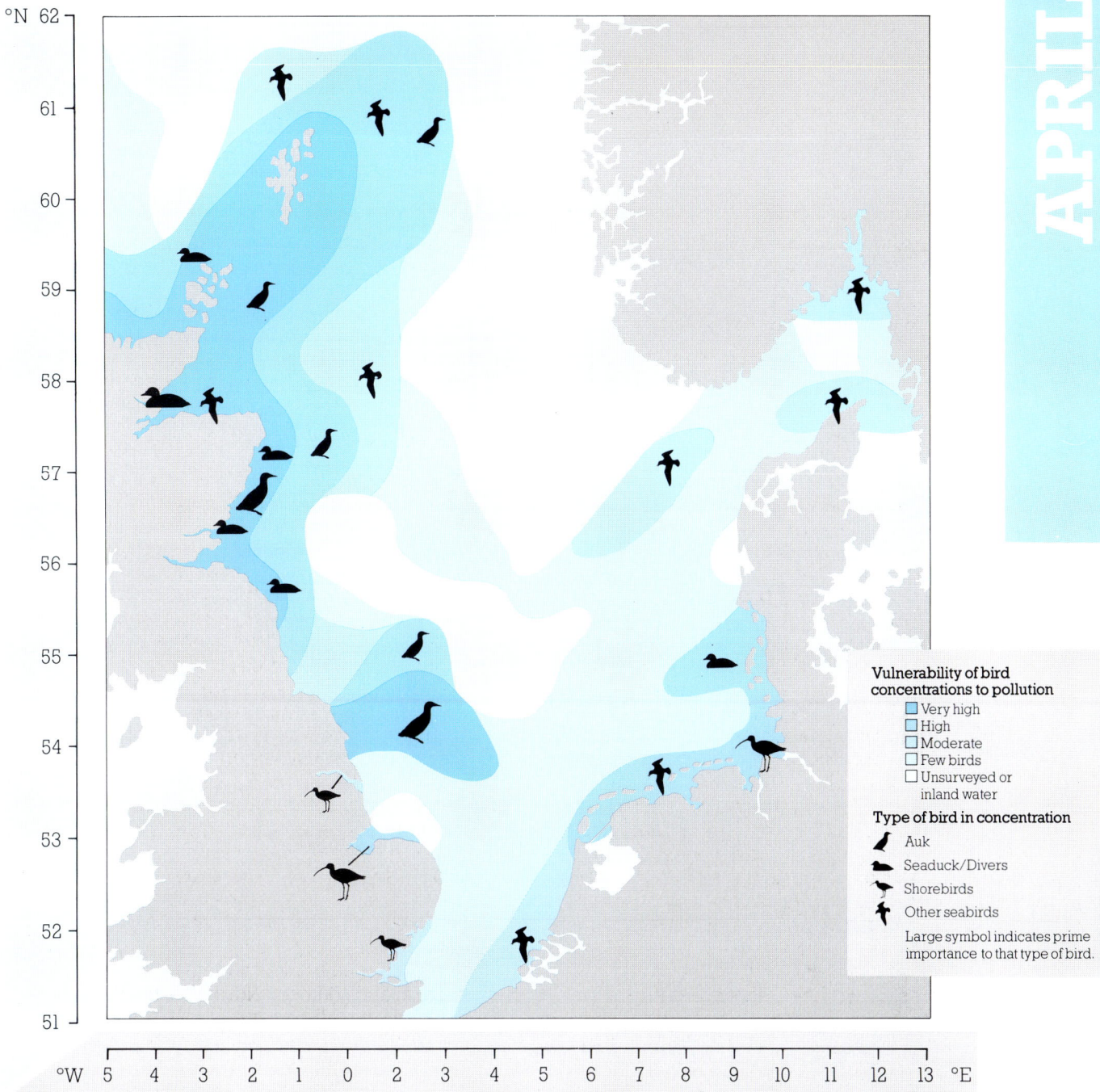

Vulnerability of bird concentrations to pollution
- Very high
- High
- Moderate
- Few birds
- Unsurveyed or inland water

Type of bird in concentration
- Auk
- Seaduck/Divers
- Shorebirds
- Other seabirds

Large symbol indicates prime importance to that type of bird.

seen around trawlers. The gull population that breeds on the shores of the Moray Firth and Firth of Forth continues to feed at sea. Movements of black-headed and little gulls are normally coastal and are evident along the eastern shores of the North Sea. The largest numbers of lesser black-backed gulls in the North Sea breed in the Skagerrak; birds arrive at the colonies during late March and April. However, relatively few birds are seen at sea.

A few arctic skuas appear in the North Sea during the month, but the most obvious arrival is that of the terns. These are seen in some numbers in the Southern Bight. Sandwich terns are the first to arrive in any numbers, followed by arctic and common, with little terns last. High densities of fulmars are seen in the extreme north-west North Sea.

Much of the Norwegian sector, the northern part of the Dogger Bank and an area off the Firth of Forth remain to be surveyed. No observations have been made off the Wash and northern Norfolk. This last area may prove important for auks as there are substantial numbers of birds a short distance to the north.

May

Inshore and coastal birds

Waders and waterfowl that wintered south of the North Sea, migrate rapidly through the Wadden Sea during the month. Most of the species moving so late nest in the high Arctic, and movement is delayed because of frozen breeding grounds. Peaks in numbers on migration occur for ringed plover, grey plover, knot, sanderling, dunlin, bar-tailed godwit and turnstone. Dark-bellied brent geese, whose numbers increased in April, reach a peak in early May before a rapid departure at the end of the month.

On British North Sea coasts only two estuaries hold internationally important flocks of birds—the Wash and the Humber. Both hold internationally important flocks of dunlin, while the former also has internationally important numbers of knot, and numbers of brent goose remain. Some estuaries with substantial tracts of saltmarshes have important numbers of breeding waders. Most wildfowl have returned to their breeding sites; on North Sea coasts these include Shetland, Orkney, Grampian, the Firth of Forth and north-east England.

The migration of divers through the North Sea continues during the month; large numbers are present off Denmark in the early part of May, before moving to their breeding grounds east of the Baltic late in the month. Numbers migrating off eastern Britain are smaller.

Offshore seabirds

Most seabirds lay their eggs and commence incubation during the month. Very few birds are present in areas away from breeding sites, and those that are in these areas are likely to be immature. The most important areas for auks are Shetland, Orkney, Caithness, Grampian, Firth of Forth, Farne Islands and Flamborough Head, Yorkshire. These birds may feed further from the colonies than in the chick-rearing period in June, and concentrations may occur up to 60 km from colonies. Kittiwakes may range somewhat further from their colonies, concentrations being found 120 km away. This has been observed particularly in the southern North Sea off Flamborough Head. Gannets range a similar distance from their colonies (Shetland and Firth of Forth).

Most summer visitors to the North Sea have returned by mid-month and are in the area of their breeding sites. New arrivals to the northern North Sea include Manx shearwater, storm petrel, arctic skua and the terns. The first two species are present in low numbers as only adult breeding birds will be present: immatures remain for a longer period in the southern wintering areas. Later in the summer larger numbers of non-breeders return to the area. Terns are found near their breeding sites; the largest proportion of Sandwich and little terns is in the southern North Sea, while the majority of arctic terns are on Shetland and Orkney. The eastern shores of the North Sea hold the largest numbers of common terns.

Very few gulls are seen at sea; the exceptions being the Moray Firth and Firth of Forth, where herring and great black-backed gulls are found, and the Skagerrak and Southern Bight, where common and lesser black-backed gulls may feed at sea. Some fulmars leave their colonies for about ten days during the first half of May and range some

Common terns

°N 62

61

60

59

58

57

56

55

54

53

52

51

°W 5 4 3 2 1 0 1 2 3 4 5 6 7 8 9 10 11 12 13 °E

Vulnerability of bird concentrations to pollution

☐ Very high
☐ High
☐ Moderate
☐ Few birds
☐ Unsurveyed or inland water

Type of bird in concentration

🐦 Auk

🐦 Seaduck/Divers

🐦 Shorebirds

🐦 Other seabirds

Large symbol indicates prime importance to that type of bird.

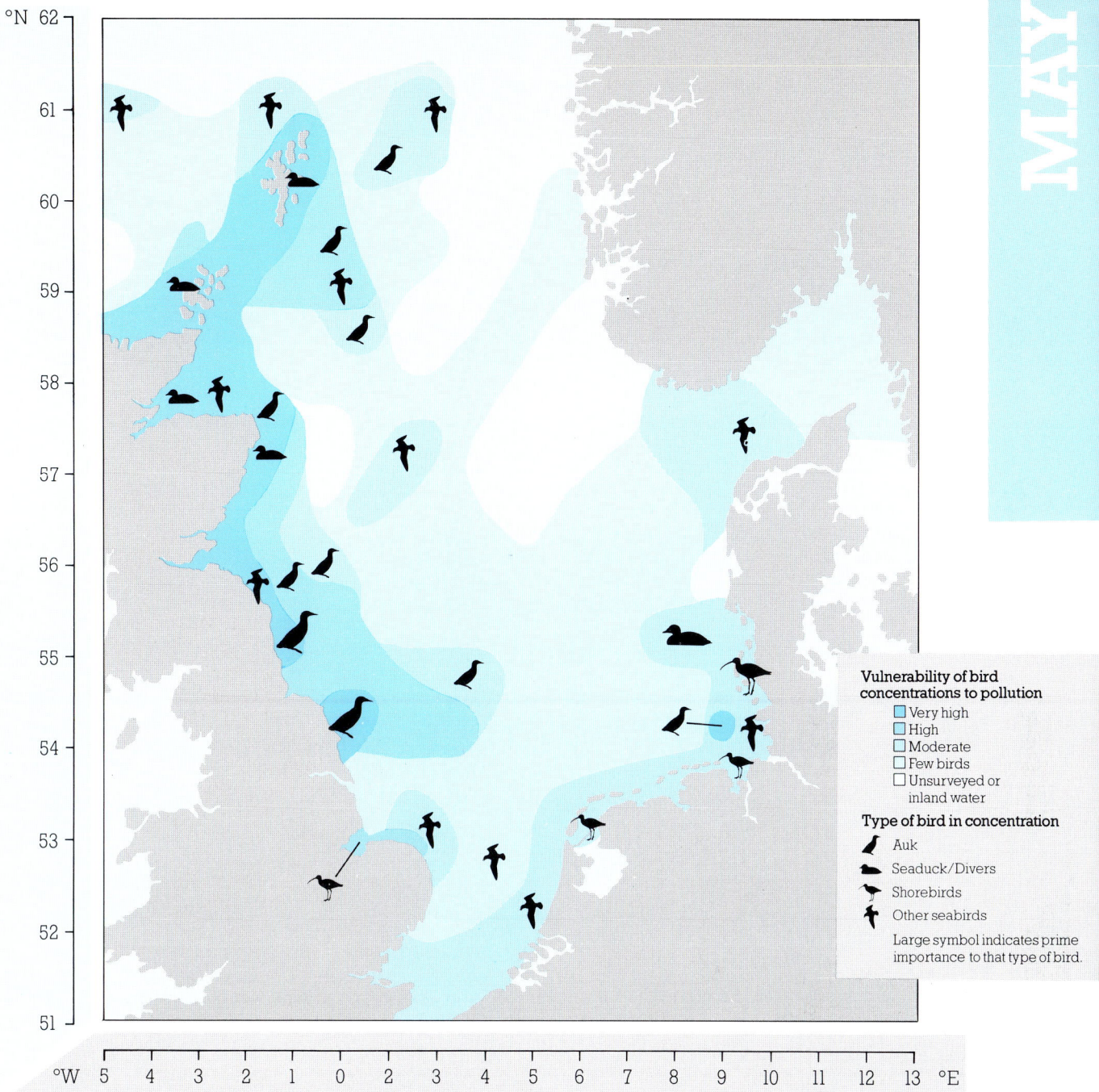

distance. This may be associated with the need to acquire sufficient protein and fat resources before egg-laying.

An area to the south-west and another to the west of Norway need to be surveyed. A small area to the east of Grampian also remains to be examined and may be important for auks.

Main additional sources of information

BLAKE, B.F., TASKER, M.L., JONES, P.H., DIXON, T.J., MITCHELL, R., & LANGSLOW, D.R. 1984. Seabird distribution in the North Sea, final report of phase 1 of the Seabirds at Sea programme. Huntingdon, Nature Conservancy Council.

CRAMP, S., BOURNE, W.R.P., & SAUNDERS, D. 1974. The seabirds of Britain and Ireland. London, Collins.

DANIELSEN, F., DURINCK, J., & SKOV, H. 1986. Biological and environmental conditions of the North Sea—mapping of conditions in Danish sector and the Wadden Sea with reference to oil spill impact. Annex A: Atlas of birds. Preliminary determination of areas important to water birds with assessment of sensitivity to oil pollution. Copenhagen, Maersk Olie og Gas A/S.

DAVIDSON, N.C., & PIENKOWSKI, M.W., eds. 1987. The conservation of international flyway populations of waders. Wader Study Group Bulletin 49, supplement, IWRB Special Publication No. 7

KING, J.G., & SANGER, G.A. 1979. Oil vulnerability index for marine oriented birds. In: Conservation of marine birds of northern north America, ed. by J.C.Bartonek and D.N.Nettleship. Washington, U.S. Department of the Interior, Fish and Wildlife Service (Wildlife Research Report No. 11).

LEE, A.J., & RAMSTER, J.W. 1981. Atlas of the seas around the British Isles. Lowestoft, Ministry of Agriculture, Fisheries and Food.

MEININGER, P.L., BAPTIST, H.J.M., & SLOB, G.J. 1984. Vogeltellingen in het Deltagebied in 1975/76—1979/80. Middelburg, Rijkswaterstaat/ Staatsbosbeheer.

MEININGER, P.L., BAPTIST, H.J.M., & SLOB, G.J. 1985. Vogeltellingen in het zuidelijk Deltagebied in 1980/81—1983/84. Middelburg, Rijkswaterstaat/ Staatsbosbeheer.

OWEN, M., ATKINSON-WILLES, G.L., & SALMON D.G. 1986. Wildfowl in Great Britain. 2nd ed. Cambridge, Cambridge University Press.

PIERSMA, T. comp. 1986. Breeding waders in Europe: a review of population size estimates and a bibliography of information sources. Wader Study Group Bulletin, 48, supplement.

PRATER, A.J. 1981. Estuary birds of Britain and Ireland. Calton, T. and A.D. Poyser.

RUGER, A., PRENTICE, C., & OWEN, M. 1986. Results of the IWRB International Waterfowl Census 1967—1983. IWRB special publ. No. 6, Slimbridge.

SMIT, C.J., & WOLFF, W.J., eds. 1981. Birds of the Wadden Sea. Final report of the Wadden Sea Working Group. Rotterdam, A.A.Balkema.

TASKER, M.L., WEBB, A., HALL, A.J., PIENKOWSKI, M.W., & LANGSLOW, D.R. 1987. Seabirds in the North Sea. Peterborough, Nature Conservancy Council (report of phase 2 of the Seabirds at Sea programme).

Wader and wildfowl counts. The results of National Wildfowl Counts and Birds of Estuaries Enquiry in the United Kingdom. These reports, edited by several authors, are published each year by the Wildfowl Trust, Slimbridge under contract with the NCC.